Busola,

Transformation begins
with you.

Romans 12:1-2

Jan. 2019

FILL YOUR GAP

7 Steps for Creating a Life of Growth, Abundance and Power

FILL YOUR GAP

7 Steps for Creating a Life of Growth, Abundance and Power

HOPELYN MULLINGS BROWN

Paperback: 978-1-64085-474-1

Hardback: 978-1-64085-475-8

Ebook: 978-1-64085-476-5

Library of Congress Cataloging 2018960069

DEDICATION

Filling your GAP is never a solo effort. For that reason this book is dedicated to all those who have impacted my life from childhood all the way to womanhood: my husband and sons, my family, my friends, my professors, business associates, my sisterhood of life coaches, and my life coaches. I also recognize those whom I have coached and trained; those I have been honored to serve, and those who have served me. To mention every person's name here would be impossible, but if you are holding this book in your hands and you have impacted my life in some way, please know that I value your contribution to my life, and I would like to hear from you. Take a moment to send me a note, so we can reconnect soon.

Transform Your Life … Transform Your World

Hopelyn

CONTENTS

Part 3: Power Your Dream --
7 Intentional Steps

ACKNOWLEDGEMENTS

To Jamaica, my motherland, where I spent the first 35 years of my life. Lessons from my teachers in all phases of my growing up years continue to offer a strong foundation for me to stand on.

To America, where I got to live the dream God planted in my mother's heart. As a young girl I read the books she received from one of her favorite ministries in America where I eventually earned my four year undergrad degree.

To Audley my husband, Jahmarley, Nick, Theo, my family, whose love gives me courage to leave a legacy that will last throughout generations.

To my beta-readers and my editor, Lonnell Johnson, you have helped me to intricately weave in the stories of my life into this powerful message of growth, abundance and power.

To my God and Creator of my life who have planted these dreams in my heart, leading me to uncover defining moments through my times of stillness to hear His voice and be guided by His Spirit.

INTRODUCTION

Be Still

"Be still, and know that I am God. I will be exalted among the nations, I will be exalted in the earth!"

~ Psalm 46:10 (KJV)

In stillness you hear the voice of your Creator. He wants to have conversation with you. Ask Him to help you glean the wisdom from the pages of this book as you read. There is great benefit in that stillness, so remain quiet and listen for His voice. He will speak to you. He might be saying, "Come closer to me" or "Come to know me." To come closer requires meditation, prayer, and study of who He is. To "come to know" requires discovering who He is and forming a relationship with Him.

Throughout this book you will be encouraged to come to know Him and come closer through understanding who you are, why you were created, and what you were called to do. You will be strengthened if you start each day spending time with Him. Asking for His guidance and direction for your life and career or business will benefit you in a great way, as you incorporate this practice into your daily living. Answers are awaiting in stillness. If you will listen attentively and journal what you hear, you will find answers to many of the questions that you have been longing to understand.

> So we can confidently say, "The Lord is my helper; I will not fear; what can man do to me?"
> ~ Hebrews 13:5-6

When you arise daily, don't forget He is near you. "I will never leave you nor forsake you." So we can confidently say, "The Lord is my helper; I will not fear; what can man do to me?" ~ Hebrews 13:5-6

• • •

According to *Inc. Magazine*, 92% of people today believe a gap is holding them back from living their dreams. *Fill Your GAP* shows how the other 8% have closed this GAP.

What would you rather do?

- Fill your GAP or let it hold you back from intentional personal **Growth**?
- Maintain a rich life or lose the motivation to live a life of **Abundance**?
- Increase your **Power** and become a person that walk confidently in this world or walk around the world with your head hung low?

When you fill your GAPs, it transforms every area of your life: Body - Soul - Spirit.

When you uncover your hurt and pain, you take the first step to filling your **GAP--G**rowth, **A**bundance and **P**ower. This act of uncovering opens moments that define the beautiful dreams among the ache and trauma and awaken you to inspire future successes.

This book provides GAP fillers to help you to become a more empowered you. Applying these keys for success and becoming more aware of the powerful messages coming from within can lead to being more equipped in your personal **G**rowth, **A**bundance, and **P**ower for a lifetime.

Having coached, trained, and spoken at workshops, seminars, and conferences, I have been honored with opportunities to help professionals and entrepreneurs from all walks of life to become their best selves. The stories they share with me are quite moving and transformational. Many attending coaching sessions in my home office or over the phone most times are stuck or feel trapped in life's circumstances. They are sometimes scared, timid, confused, and lack direction and purpose. They feel worthless, hopeless, and lonely. They want to give up. They are ready for change, and they want guidance. They have an inkling that there is more, and they need help to find it. As their coach, I am delighted to say that 90% or more of those I have worked with leave their coaching sessions feeling more hopeful, confident, courageous, and ready to effect change in their lives. As a result, they positively impact their families and organizations.

Fill Your GAP is about letting go of the hurt and pain and awakening to growth, abundance, and power. It will help you take the circumstances life has given you from these aches and traumas, and use them as a springboard to persevere through life. Knowing this can help those who desire to fill those GAPs that were caused by setbacks they experienced.

You may find similarities in the life story of someone mentioned in this book. The stories included share how each person opened up fully to the coaching process and was able to fill their GAP—growth, abundance, and power; by identifying the pain points that were holding them back and using intentional steps that I guided them through which led to discovery and empowerment. The pain points were there as guides to help these entrepreneurs and professionals discover for sure what they were called to do in this world. A new perspective toward those experiences guided them to growth with purpose, clarity in the passions of their lives, and confidence to overcome the setbacks they encountered. In turn they became empowered to live the life of their dreams.

As you apply these steps daily, weekly, monthly, and yearly; the missing pieces will begin to come together for a more complete or beautiful picture. These steps are designed to bring clarity to your mind regarding the direction of your life as you look forward to your future. As you read this book, consider it as a tool to help you build a solid foundation for your life, family, career, business, and wherever else you have influence.

PART 1
THE GROWTH PROCESS -- AWAKEN YOUR DREAMS

The beautiful dreams within you may have been hidden far too long. This is the opportunity to awaken hidden potential to lead you to future successes. The stages of the butterfly life cycle provide a great parallel to awakening hidden dreams. A complete metamorphosis is necessary to live an empowered life of purpose and abundance.

Uncovering your hurts and pain is the first step to increasing your **G**rowth, **A**bundance, and **P**ower. As you uncover painful memories, you will also discover defining moments that unveil the beautiful dreams and awaken your heart to amazing possibilities. Additional steps to personal Growth, Abundance, and Power include learning to be still and listening to spiritual messages coming from within. Keep in mind the introduction to "Be Still."

CHAPTER 1
AWAKE FROM SLEEPING

"If every day is an awakening, you will never grow old. You will just keep growing."

Gail Sheehy

Morning by morning he awakens; he awakens my ear to hear as those who are taught.

~ Isaiah 50:4

Begin the awakening journey with me as I share some of the defining moments that transformed my life. I am still on this journey of purpose as my transformation takes on more color, expands further and grows deeper every day. Relax and read this part of my story over a cup of tea—you may need more than a cup, depending on how quickly you read.

Humble beginnings...

Being born at home, I was known as a home baby. I came into this world, thanks to my mother's midwife, Nurse Rose. *May her soul rest in peace*. This journey of life could not have been if there had not been a caring team of people at the start to ensure I was delivered safely and mindfully nurtured to maturity. This part of our lives is sometimes taken for granted. *Take a moment to reflect on your early beginnings*.

I remember returning to the community where I lived for most of my growing up years in Jamaica. In November 2007, I decided to visit that little "board" house where I was born—a small house made with a concrete foundation and a wooden frame. It was still there! Old, but still standing. What a nostalgic moment.

I grew up in Bull Bay, St. Andrew, with my siblings: six sisters and three brothers. Sadly, my sister, Stephanie, passed away in 2002 from breast cancer, and I was honored to become mother to her only son, Jahmarley. I became a single parent during that season of my life and was blessed to parent him with my husband shortly after my nephew, Jahmarley, legally became my son.

My mother, Joyce Mullings, is still alive and aging well for the most part. My father died on June 18, 2018 at the age of eighty-one after aging rapidly over a one year period. *May his soul rest in peace*.

Our family grew up with Christian values, and we attended a local Pentecostal church where we were initially invited in to get shelter from the rain back in the early 1960s. A small group of people were initiating the launch of a new church in the area, and on this particular Sunday afternoon, my mother found a place to help her lay a solid foundation for her family. This became our family church, and I attended regularly with my parents and siblings.

I was born in 1961, the second & third child to my parents. Let me explain. I was the second child for both my parents and the third for one parent who had another child before they both got married. I hope that brings some clarity. My mother shared with me recently about the nights she was at home alone in the one-bedroom home. Many nights she had to stand up in the middle of the bed, chasing scorpions off the wall in that little starter home she and my father built for their family.

In the 1970s, I experienced a form of trauma from abuse of a close family member, and the sense of confusion within me sometimes forced me to sleep more than I should have or go into hiding. My actions caused my mother great concern, but I did not understand what I was going through, much less how to express it to her.

> "Be still, and know that I am God. I will be exalted among the nations, I will be exalted in the earth!" ~ Psalm 46:10

The memories of the girl being abused are quite different pictures compared to the many flashbacks of dreams I have had while playing in the yard with my siblings and friends. These were dreams I had awakened to after a good night's sleep or daydreaming. These memories excite me for the most part because they inspire me to live beyond the pain and trauma I had experienced during those earlier years that would want to hold me back from pursuing my best life.

Awaken Your Dreams

Begin to think about your dreams. Dreams you had as a child. Dreams you have or have had for your family. Your dream vacation spots that you long to visit. Dreams you had for your career or business. When you think of them, do they make you light up? Do you feel a sense of joy? Do you feel hopeful? Let these dreams propel you to pursuing your best life.

Applying the steps outlined in this book will unveil defining moments from your dreams that you can draw lessons from. You can then process and bring them to life. This act will empower you to create a life worth living.

To start your journey, purchase a new journal or use the *Fill Your GAP* note pages at the end of this book. Set aside writing time each day to begin uncovering your thoughts. During this activity, list all your dreams as they come to mind. Spend time in regular reflection and add to your story. Keeping your journal close at hand, you can add new thoughts as you give birth to fresh ideas and new dreams.

You will create a strategic plan to bring your dream to life. This means creating goals around your dreams and beginning to take action in anticipation of exceptional personal growth. Think about the life cycle of the caterpillar becoming a butterfly. Bringing your dreams to life is a step-by-step process, completed in such a way that it does not compromise the next step. This progressive process requires moving outside of your comfort zone and taking risks. It has been said "Without risks there are no rewards." It's time to reap some rewards by creating a successful action plan to fill your GAP. I know you desire more in your life, and you are now ready for this challenge.

As you progress on this journey to fill your GAP, you will encounter new concepts and ideas presented in a simple format to make it easy to implement. Remember, keep a steady pace, pause to smell the roses or process a step in the path, and then move on. The journey will have its challenges, so use the step-by-step guide to have a safe journey of Growth, Abundance and Power.

As you progress in your journey, you will encounter terms used in Fill Your GAP to help you understand some of the challenges and triumphs awaiting you. Know that there will be GAP stealers along your journey. Being ready with GAP fillers will help move you along at a greater pace. Here are some GAP stealers and GAP fillers for you to be aware of. We will discuss these in greater details later.

GAP Stealers—ungratefulness, hate, ignorance, foolishness, entitlement, despair, arrogance, condemnation, self-interest, and fear.

GAP Fillers—gratefulness/appreciation, love, knowledge, wisdom, hard work, hope, humility, and service.

Looking back on my life, this community and church family helped to set a firm foundation for me to understand family, discipline, love, and honor among many of the values I hold dear. Your values form your foundation. It is so important that you examine your values as you go through different seasons of your life. In Chapter 9 Map Out Your GAP, Step 4, you will find a Values Assessment to help you examine or establish your values to create a solid foundation in your life. Pause to reflect for a moment with the questions below before reading further.

Chapter Reflections:

What are some of the GAP stealers you have identified in your life as you read this chapter?

_____

_____

_____

What are some of the GAP fillers you can replace those GAP stealers with?

_____

_____

_____

How have Dr. Brown's experiences inspired you?

_____

_____

_____

CHAPTER 2
CAPTURE DEFINING MOMENTS

"My great concern is not whether you have failed, but whether you are content with your failure."

~ Abraham Lincoln

"For I know the plans I have for you," declares the Lord, *"plans to prosper you and not to harm you, plans to give you hope and a future."*

~ Jeremiah 29:11

In 1981 my high school boyfriend had returned to Jamaica from Canada for a short visit. He and one of our high school friends surprised me at my place of work. I was overjoyed to reconnect with him. We enjoyed the time spent together, yet we never expressed the true love we had in our hearts for each other. Twenty-two years later, he found me and expressed what he would have wanted to do on his visit in 1981. Over those missing years, as he would call it, I persevered through broken relationships yet remained strong and kept on pursuing my life dreams.

My mother is a spiritually strong woman, and I inherently have embraced her perseverance and spiritual heritage. Fond and reverent recollections of my mother praying for all of us, walking from room to room in the middle of the night and praying, still touch me deeply. I remember just lying there awake, without her knowing, just listening in awe to her as she prayed for me, the rest of my siblings, and my family as a whole. I am convinced I received my "warrior" spirit from my mother. Now it makes me smile to think of it. Her prayers made me feel safe, and they brought great comfort. This defining moment still allows me to feel that safety throughout my life, knowing that even today my mama is still praying for me.

> Our Creator — God — has great plans for your life!

His heart is expressed in these words from Bible: "For I know the plans I have for you, says the LORD, plans for welfare and not for evil, to give you a future and a hope." (Jeremiah 29:11—Revised Standard Version)

A hope and great future await you. Living in today's world will challenge that truth as you pursue the journey to fully grow into who God created you to be. The cultures of this world bombard you from every angle with conflicting messages, and without a guide you can be led down the wrong path.

This hope for the future, the expectation that there's a great future awaiting you, will help you lay a solid foundation for your life, family, career, business, and wherever you have influence. Hope also brings clarity to the development of your GAP -- **Growth, Abundance and Power.**

Growth

Growth in your life can also refer to developing or maturing physically, mentally, or spiritually. For example, keeping a

> "There are no new ideas. There are only new ways of making them felt." ~ Audre Lord

journal can be a vital step in our personal growth. Time set aside to reflect, process, contemplate and envision can lead to more awareness of your individual development leading to a life change.

Have you ever heard the expression used by Tony Robbins?: "If you do what you've always done, you'll get what you've always gotten"? Something needs to change. We can't expect to get better results if we're not willing to change how we do things. Growth requires personal progress. You need to take action in order to see change in your personal growth, but the challenge is how do you make the change? You want a better tomorrow. You have desires, dreams, and hopes. Maybe you have a habit you want to break, or a goal you want to reach, or a skill you want to develop. Growth is made up of incremental changes. I want to help you develop the right attitude, learn more about your strengths, tap into your passion, become more in touch with your purpose, and develop your skills so you can be all you can be.

Abundance

"If you help people get what they want, they will help you get what you want." ~ Zig Ziglar

Abundance is defined as an extremely plentiful or over-sufficient quantity or supply:

For example, an abundance of grain, or overflowing fullness: abundance of the heart.

It's also referred to as affluence; wealth: the enjoyment of abundance.

When most people hear the word abundance, they begin to question it as if it has negative connotations. There seem to be a fear around this word abundance. Do you desire to live a good life? Begin to define abundance in your own terms. It's time to escape your scarcity mindset, challenge your beliefs, and commit to leaving a meaningful impact on this planet. Unfortunately, we were all brought up to believe there's only so much pie. Our parents, teachers, and society as a whole taught us there's only so much to go around. This is not the truth! You have a unique calling in your life waiting for you to come forth and express it in its abundance so you can flourish in this world. God provides you with everything you need to do, all He has called you to do. You are abundantly equipped to fulfill your unique destiny.

Power

"Mastering others is strength. Mastering yourself is true power." ~ Tao Te Ching

Power is defined as the ability to do or act. The capability of doing or accomplishing something would be another definition. Do you realize you were born with power? Your Creator gave you the ability to think, to understand, to reason, to sense, to feel and the determination and self-discipline to take action. All of these abilities work in harmony to strengthen your life and give you the power to manage your thoughts and emotions rather than letting them be controlled by outside circumstances. Power is the combined strength of three forces: your spirit, wisdom, and determination coming together and causing your life to flourish, even in the midst of challenging circumstances. With personal power you are able to choose:

- Love over hate
- Courage over fear
- Hope over despair
- Wisdom over foolishness
- Knowledge over ignorance
- Appreciation over ungratefulness
- Humility over arrogance
- Hard work over entitlement
- Grace over condemnation
- Service over self-interest

Chapter seven goes deeper into the topic of GAP Fillers and Stealers. Stay alert and stay filled with love, courage, hope, wisdom, knowledge, appreciation, humility, hard work, grace, and service.

Before you move ahead, take a moment to assess where you are today. This self-assessment is an important tool to help you to honestly assess where you are at today and guide you to your new future with more hope and confidence.

Complete the Self-assessment sheet to gain some clarity on where you are today in your personal or professional life. *(Notice that the questions are personalized for you)*

Self-assessment Questions:

1. What is currently going well in my life and career/business?

   _____

   _____

   _____

2. What is currently not going well in my life and career/ business?

   _____

   _____

   _____

3. What changes MUST I make to move from where I am today to where I desire to be in my life and career/business?

   _____

   _____

   _____

Now that you have completed your self-assessment, you should have greater clarity on where you desire to go from here. The next step you take will be a bit smoother as you continue this process.

Take a look at how you are influencing others and you will become more aware of your personal values. This values exercise is another step in building a solid foundation for your future. You will get the opportunity to delve deeper.

Go at your own pace. Take all the steps necessary to bring your personal growth and development to the next level.

Start with a small step and do not force the stage you are in.

Simply ensure your steps are completed to the best of your ability. When you look closely inside a caterpillar's hard outer shell or cocoon; in that stage of development, you can actually see the tiny butterfly growing inside--the chrysalis. This is what happens when you are awakening your dream. You will have to deal with the challenges as the butterfly deals with all the external elements coming against it. Chapter five talks about how you prepare your foundation and build up reinforcements to ensure you do not fail.

My foundational values came about by observing my mother

Do not try to be a perfectionist.

who was a hard worker. I remember how she worked right up to her due dates during her pregnancies. When she had stopped having children, she began travelling to the United States to work. After seeing the opportunities available there, she decided her children would have better educational and career opportunities, so she filed for us to become American residents.

I loved my life in Jamaica and was resolute in my decision that the only way I would go to the USA would be if I was granted the opportunity to pursue a university degree. My increased longing to pursue higher education since I left high school was the driving force in making the final decision to leave Jamaica for the USA. I had a strong leaning toward mentoring those who were on the verge of losing hope, and after training to develop greater skills, I sought to help them with the knowledge and wisdom I had gained.

When others whom you respect have an opinion of how you should live your dreams, you want to listen, don't you? I recall sharing my plans about relocating for the purposes of higher education with a former manager with whom I worked , and he said, "You are making enough money and in a comfortable job and your career is booming. Why stop now?" With all of this success that was clear, I could not deny the disquiet in my spirit. After about a year of pondering, I resigned from my successful career in the life insurance industry and boarded a plane for Brooklyn, New York in April 1995. I took with me two suitcases of as much of my possessions as I could pack to begin this new season of my life.

Brooklyn was not at all as glamorous as my friends, family, as well as portrayals in movies and other TV shows made it out to be. As quickly as I arrived, I desperately desired to get out of that city. For survival purposes, I pursued job opportunities and secured several positions almost immediately. These jobs were in three different locations. In Brooklyn, I was asked to sit in as a care aide for an elderly couple in Manhattan. I also obtained a job with an airline company to handle reward points in their customer service division and in a non- profit organization as a scribe to address envelopes for an upcoming charity function. I also worked with World Book Products in book sales, knocking from door-to-door in the suburbs of Brooklyn, New Jersey, and Queens selling encyclopedias. I enjoyed working with World Book Products because I had the opportunity to encourage and assist mothers and families within these communities to obtain resources for their children and family education.

While pursuing these opportunities, my focus to go to college did not wane. I sought out colleges and completed and mailed out applications. About three months after arriving in Brooklyn, I was accepted into the Oral Roberts University (ORU) in Tulsa, Oklahoma. I was overjoyed! In July 1995, I boarded the Greyhound bus, the only source of transportation I could afford, and headed to Tulsa, Oklahoma to begin college that summer semester.

Why Oral Roberts University? I had no intentions of heading to ORU, much less Tulsa, Oklahoma! When I had arrived in Brooklyn from Jamaica, I connected with a Jamaican friend who was a graduate of ORU. We spend quite a bit of time catching up on the years we were apart. One afternoon I was telling my friend about the challenges I was having with my college applications, and she recommended ORU. I found it strange that I was getting no response from applications sent to other colleges and universities in and around New York. I decided to take a chance and apply to ORU, and to my surprise, they were the first to respond. My family and friends thought I was losing my mind to go to ORU, which was so far away and in the "middle of nowhere." But I made up my mind.

What idea or dream have you made up your mind about, but you are feeling discouraged? Search deeply to uncover what ignited that idea or dream and go back there to find strength to move to the next step of your journey.

In retrospect, I now understand that going to ORU in Tulsa, Oklahoma was my mother's dream. As a partner of Oral Roberts Ministry, she had always desired for one of her children to attend ORU, and now that desire was being fulfilled. My mother knew that based on the household income, it would have been unaffordable to send me off to college after my graduation from high school back in 1978, so she made efforts to apply for a scholarship but had received no success at that time. Little did she know that God had a plan!

My steps are ordered...

My bus trip from New York to Oklahoma lasted almost two days. It was destiny that while I was still living in Jamaica and attending my home church, Fellowship Tabernacle; I met and became good friends with Madeline Manning Mims, who had come to visit Jamaica and minister at our church there. Madeline is the first and only American female to win an Olympic gold medal in the 800-meter event, accomplishing this feat in Mexico City in 1968. My church was getting ready to open our newly formed Theater House, and Madeline was invited as a special guest singer/speaker at its launch. I was the designated hospitality hostess for Madeline, and we became fast friends. We had kept in touch; therefore, she was aware of my plans to attend ORU. Madeline resided in Tulsa then, and she and her family met me at the bus station in Tulsa, OK. They hosted me in their home before I could settle comfortably in a studio apartment I was renting in close proximity to the college campus. For me this was a season filled with defining moments.

Chapter Reflections:

What are some personal defining moments you have identified in your life as you read this chapter?

_____

_____

_____

How will you use these defining moments to fuel your goal pursuit?

_____

_____

_____

How have Dr. Brown's experiences inspired you?

_____

_____

_____

CHAPTER 3

ESTABLISH YOUR FOUNDATION

""We are what we repeatedly do. Excellence, then, is not an act but a habit"

~ Aristotle

"Therefore, everyone who listens to these messages of mine and puts them into practice is like a wise man who built his house on a rock."

~ Matthew 7:24

Though I grew up with a solid spiritual foundation, I would find myself seeking to understand the worldly things that were appealing to my senses. For a season of about ten years I searched for deeper meaning in my relationship with God, yet at the same time explored other ways of life that I was not exposed to in my earlier years. I partied with my friends and enjoyed revelry yet felt a deep sense of discontentment after my encounters. Looking back, I am glad that my foundation created in the earlier years of my life stood strong.

Foundations are built to last forever. Take the foundation of a home. My father was a contractor/builder in my growing up years, so my siblings and I participated in the building of our childhood home. I remember how long it took to build the foundation of the different sections of the home before he started laying the bricks over the steel frames in the foundation. Considerable time was spent prior on digging and removing debris, stones, and anything else to create a levelled area and prepare the ground for the building of our home. Day after day we would work together and see each section of our home come to life before our own eyes. Today that house that was built almost 60 years ago still stands on that foundation.

Laying the foundation to fill your GAP will require more time and effort at the beginning to ensure that it last forever. This is the reason your aches and pain must be uprooted and dealt with as you delve into personal growth and development. The pain buried alive does not bring about healing. It can erode the foundation of your life at a time you least expect it. Unmasking the pain leads to defining moments and exposes the amazing plans in store for your future self.

The Lifecycle of the Butterfly

This poem developed that Dr. Scott and Joan Simmerman of PerformanceManagementCompanyBlog. com introduces paradoxical concepts associated with the life cycle of the butterfly:

Imagine two caterpillars looking on
As a beautiful butterfly floats on by
One turns saying, after it is gone,
"Not ever me as a butterfly that high!"

Push away Resistance and be open for Change.
STOP and be more than just a caterpillar, ho hum.
Start by envisioning ideas beyond your range
And gain The Answer to what you can become.

As with the Caterpillar, it could be a gooey mess
But you'll improve and gain self-esteem, for sure
Change is about letting go, trusting the process
Of becoming more than you are with things you were.

The caterpillar was quite resistant and content,
Causing him to ignore what the change involved.
He thought his answer would stop the event—
His Mother is a moth—his problem was solved!

Can we all learn from this? What can we try?
Fight it as we might, Change will come our way
The caterpillar's colors are in and on the butterfly
We, too, can transform with our colors still in play.

The lifecycle of the butterfly is one of the most fascinating phenomenon in all of Nature. The different stages of the butterfly relate closely to your personal and professional growth. Consider these three stages and see how you can apply the lessons to your own development.

Stage 1: The Caterpillar

This stage which follows right after hatching from an egg, and the object at this point is nourishment. The caterpillar's task is solely to consume as much as possible to fuel the future growth. Throughout this stage the caterpillar will outgrow and shed its skin as many as four or five times.

This stage represents the learning stage in personal growth: taking time to read books, listening to videos and audios, attending seminars, workshops, and conferences. These events help you to consume as much knowledge and training as you can to understand and master yourself. Aligning yourself with a life coach and tribe of people who will support you in your personal growth journey can be beneficial. This connection brings additional fuel to propel your growth. By observing others who have mastered what you are seeking to master, you can receive authentic, applicable, and life-changing guidance. During this stage there is "shedding" of old habits and ideas that you will need to walk away from. Partaking of the personal development outlets contributes to a greater flow of creativity and inspiration. You will experience a sense of euphoria at this stage as you shed the old and embrace the anticipation of the next season of your life, both personally and/or professionally.

Stage 2: The Chrysalis

This intriguing stage of butterfly development would seem to lead to tragic experience from the caterpillar's view. Having been nourished in stage one, the caterpillar is now fully grown and has reached its capacity in taking in all the nourishment it can get. At this point, it attaches itself to a solid branch and creates a protective covering or chrysalis around itself to withdraw and stay protected while it digests the food consumed in stage one. During this stage the chrysalis appears unchanged on the outside, though there is phenomenal transformation taking place inside. This is where the body of the caterpillar is slowly degenerating while the dormant cells of the emerging butterfly are slowly awakening to join together and create a brand new being.

As you grow into your own process of development, this stage can be quite confusing. The tendency is to ignore the need for rest, relaxation, and remaining in the right environment. When you are going through a period of personal growth or working on creating something new, it's important to understand these three factors: the need for rest, relaxation, and being in the right atmosphere. These three conditions provide inspiration, motivation, and momentum to push your growth forward. It's important not to take the perspective of this stage being dreadful and tragic because this will enhance your growth or kill your dream.

Stage 3: The Butterfly

At this third and final stage, the fully developed butterfly is ready to spread its wings and emerge from the chrysalis. When the butterfly breaks free, its wings are still folded and wet, requiring more time for rest so blood can circulate into the wings. Finally when the wings are fully dry, the butterfly is all set to take flight and begin to share its beauty with the world.

This stage requires intentional steps for "breaking free" from your chrysalis in an appropriate timeline so your "flight" is a successful one. Having gone through the other stages prepares you to launch your new self or project to the world, leaving behind old ways of accomplishing tasks and moving forward with courage and confidence. You must exercise caution during this stage you are venturing into new territories with your new "wings."

> "The LORD God gives me the right words to encourage the weary. Each morning he awakens me eager to learn his teaching;" ~ Isaiah 50:4 (Contemporary English Version)

You have awakened your dream, and you need to push through the pain in all the stages of your discovery of "Who Am I?" Awakening will open your eyes to the amazing possibilities connected to your purpose. There is no reason for allowing the labels given by the people in your life and those moments of despair to continue to interfere with the realization of your dreams.

Consider this...

Who are the people who made the path clear for you to walk or run on? Those who help to create a path in your growth journey are key to what your future will look like. My parents, teachers, spiritual leaders, and friends have impacted my life significantly for the good during specific seasons. I will highlight a few of them here:

I attended this early childhood church school from the age of three to six years old, and Aunt Ruth was my Basic School teacher. Though her classroom was filled with 50 - 60 little boys and girls, she made me feel like I was the only one in her classroom every day, She treated each one of us as special, and she identified me as a leader to keep the kids in the classroom saying their timetables and ABCs when she had to step out of the classroom for a short break.

Les Brown was one of the main speakers at an annual Million Dollar Round Table conference I qualified to attend in the USA. Back then I was living in Kingston, Jamaica and working for one of the top Life Insurance companies there. Les Brown made a great impact on me when he came on stage and delivered his famous speech "You Gotta Be Hungry." I felt it in my bones. My desire to continue rising to the top in the Life Insurance industry and then transitioning to a world renowned motivational speaker began right there in that stadium in Chicago.

Raymond Walker, the leader/manager I chose to take the plunge with in the Life Insurance industry, also influenced me in an unforgettable way. He treated all his four new recruits, of which I was included, as family. We studied together, trained together, took exams together, had breakfast together, ran on the beach together, set goals together, became a force to be reckoned with, and formed a bond like no other team. I believe this was the secret to our success. Building a strong family and team spirit that was unbreakable.

Bill Winston, Dean of The School of Leadership and my professor mentor heading the practicum as I completed my MBA, took time to help answer questions not in my awareness until he initiated them. One morning as I was meeting with him to review the work I had completed so far that week, he asked "What are your plans after graduation?" It was the same plan I had in mind after I completed my Bachelor's in Social Work--to return to Jamaica and start a home of HOPE there. We had an enlightening conversation that led to my making the decision to complete my Doctorate in Strategic Leadership.

Bramwell Osula championed me during my years of doctoral studies and guided me in remarkable ways. With his support I was able to complete my degree in the four-year time frame I had set out to accomplish. He helped me navigate through the grief and loss of my sister, and taking on the role of single parent to Jahmarley to successfully complete my Strategic Leadership studies.

Jahmarley Grant, my nephew, became my son after my younger sister, Stephanie, passed away. She was diagnosed with breast cancer at age 25, and at age 31 she succumbed to its effects. Jahmarley has been a tremendous joy in my life and though we have had our growing pains dealing with grief and loss, dealing with custody matters, dealing with single-parenting, among other life happenings, I am forever grateful for having him as my son and hearing him call me 'mother.'

Bonnie Ewasko Giesbrecht took me under her wings when I relocated to Canada in 2004. Without question, she treated me as her own sister. We baked apple pies together in her kitchen. We had family meals together. She introduced me to her church family who also took me under their wings. Something she did brought me indescribable joy: she accepted the invitation to be the matron of honor at my wedding. This season of my life was brighter because of her kindness and love.

So many other significant individuals have helped me on this journey. Leonie Wallace and Joy Wansley are among other life sisters with whom I have a deep and incredible bond that cannot be broken.

What is the foundation you are standing on?

Your foundational values manifest how you show up in the world.

Chapter Reflections:

When you consider these three stages of the butterfly, which stage would you say you are in? Explain why.

_____

_____

_____

What lessons will you apply to your own personal and professional growth?

_____

_____

_____

CHAPTER 4
DETERMINE YOUR DESTINATION

"All you need is the plan, the road map, and the courage to press on to your destination."

~ Earl Nightingale

"Strip down, start running – and never quit! No extra spiritual fat, no parasitic sins. Keep your eyes on Jesus, who both began and finished the race we're in."

~Hebrews 12:1 MSG

In 1977 as I prepared for my high school exams, the burning desire within me was to apply to nursing school and get away from home to start that new season of my life. I committed to my studies and received extra support for Math which was challenging for me, yet when the results came out, I was greatly disappointed. Es, Ds, Cs and one B! What will I do now? I resorted to my old way of escape--sleeping a lot or going into hiding. After a few weeks I made the decision to find a job and take classes to retake these exams. Thank God for Reverend Perrin, our school Chaplin, who encouraged me at that time and helped me to refocus and get back on track.

You are now ready to spread your wings, but do you know your destination? What has been that burning desire you have been holding on to for so long? What do you dream about, sing about, laugh about, cry about, or dance about? You have thought about it, wrote about it, talked about it yet done nothing about it. You have allowed the past mistakes you made, voices of descent, challenges and setbacks, and your own lack of fortitude to have held you back from pursuing your burning desire.

Think of yourself holding on to the weight of all your life's challenges. Imagine that they are all being held in a large suitcase with no handle to pull, so you have had to hoist this load on your back to carry it. You are all bent over and almost touch the ground from the weight of this luggage, yet you keep hanging on to it. It's time to surrender that weight. You cannot carry it. Surrender your weaknesses, failures, shortcomings, and lack. When you come to a place where you can let all of it go, you will open the door to greatness. You have to recognize that these areas are dead and you need help to become restored. This is a time of surrender. Allowing your ego to get in the way will cause you to deny your weaknesses, called the "dead areas" of your life. There is no benefit in that. You will have to be open to recognize these "dead areas." Daily you must surrender those weaknesses and consistently replace them with your strengths.

You may be asking, "How do I surrender? I've been trying to let go of this weight for so long! And it's going nowhere!" *"And throwing off everything that hinders us and especially the sin that so easily entangles us, let us keep running with endurance the race set before us,"* (Hebrews 12:1 ISV)

To help you in the surrender exercise complete Step 4 in Chapter 9 Map out your GAP. This will guide you through the process and release steps.

This is a story from one of my clients who totally surrendered. This is a dedication to her and although I have not used her real name and have altered some of the details to protect her privacy, I want to honor her and the strong commitment she had to her own growth and success. She was one who came to her coaching sessions with me fully engaged and ready to take it all in. I loved working with her and seeing the amazing transformation that took place in her life.

One of her friends shared with me,

"Tiffany was an amazing friend and always inspired those she came in contact with in so many ways. Her generous, selfless, loving spirit was known by those in her circle as well as the total stranger. She found humor in everything, and her friends loved that about her. Those happy memories and great love were constantly felt, even though she was not around. Her heart's mission was to make a difference and spread God's love. Tiffany lived life with an effervescent and tangible passion for Christ. It permeated her being, and she was able to connect with ANYONE because of her unconditional love for others. She would send scripture texts to her friends every day. She would share her faith with her instructors at the university. She was witnessed turning the other cheek even when any other person would fight back.

Some time ago while Tiffany and friends were at the Washington Bridge Pedal, thousands of kids, parents, and adults were bicycling across Washington's Bridges. While pedaling along, someone noticed she had pulled off to the side of the road. There was a sea of bicyclists riding by, so they had to keep going. Eventually they were able to pull out and make their way back to where Tiffany was. There they found her hugging a strange man who was sitting on the ground hurt. He had fallen and cut his arm badly. She offered him her water and was assuring him that we would provide him help. This kindness she showed distracted him from the pain, and he was smiling". This is a further testament to her authentic, loving and kind personality.

Here is Tiffany's story as she shares it.

We all have journeys in this life specific to us. They are planned by the Lord as He is the author and finisher of our faith (Hebrews 12:2). Jeremiah 29:11 declares that "God's plans for us are good; they bring us a hope and a future." So that we may see His plan for us, Proverbs 3:5-6 states that we must trust in the Lord with all our hearts as we seek His will in all we do. Upon this faith-filled assignment, God promises to show us which path to take. I know that one gift He continues to grow within all of us is the gift of faith. He revealed to me in 2008 that with this strong faith, He plans to use me to heal women hurt by abuse. When He revealed His plan for me, I wept with joy and excitement, yet soon asked, "How, Lord?" My discovery of just how to live out this plan is a journey in itself as it continually teaches me to take life one day at a time. Just with His perfect will, God has a perfect time and place for everything. The duty is mine to walk obediently in faith through the doors He methodically opens. My journey begins with a small seed of faith that grows so as to heal a great multitude. For as long as I can remember, I wanted to help the wounded and ease their pain. My hopes began with a plan to become a pediatrician; I loved children and surely did not wish for any to suffer. As I completed high school, however, I examined the professional strain in pediatrics, along with the time, money, and effort I would devote in order to earn my desired degree.

As I centered all these aspects into one focused view, I felt I did not have the confidence to become a medical leader nor did I have the motivation to obtain the degree needed for such a proficient role at the time. I look back now, and I see that Pediatrics was not the goal God intended for me anyway. Yes, He designed a different plan, and He knew seven years would pass before I became ready to hear His divine plan. These years, after all, were part of His design for my journey. He not only shaped within me the faith and motivation for my success but further, the personal understanding that I, as a leader, must possess so as to incorporate a nurturing hand to my clients.

In 2002, I decided to enter college for a simple practical nursing license with certainty that I made a better assistant than a leader. While I entered my third year in the educational process, a neurological hindrance emerged inside my right temporal lobe. Before I could understand or even discover the label of this problem, I could only see the limitations it caused in earning my degree. The directors in my nursing program soon recommended I voluntarily leave school after my grade point average descended to 3.02. I was overwhelmed with feelings that I had chosen the wrong degree completely. Although fog entered my view of career goals, I did keep my hope that God had a divine purpose for my life.

After I shared the disheartening news with the woman who provided a room for me while I attended school, she reminded me that our agreement only stood during my time in school. Now that I could no longer call myself a student, she could no longer call me her roommate and soon dismissed me from her home. Although, fear of no longer having a place to live entered my heart, God soon rescued me with shelter inside a doctor's home. Along with a room, this doctor provided a monthly income for my care of her two young boys, and the encouragement to return to school for medical assisting as a "foot in the door" to possibly earning my nursing degree later in life. Not only did this opportunity rescue me from destitution and failure, but it rescued me from death as well.

By the winter of 2005, the neurological hindrance severely increased and caused me to lose consciousness for an estimate of nine hours. If the Lord had not sheltered me inside that doctor's home, I doubt I would have been found that day, and, therefore, be alive today. In the hospital, I regained consciousness and learned that epilepsy was the term and reason for the neurological disturbances I experienced for the last year and a half. Regardless of such an intense diagnosis, the Lord blessed me with reassurance that it would not hinder the plans He designed me to accomplish.

The following three years were a time to of growth in trusting my God's strength and direction. My faith in Him, in His love, and in His healing grew abundantly. My desire that others who face similar burdens can know the freedom of Christ's love and power followed. In 2008, the fog began to lift as the Lord confirmed He placed in me the desire for healing wounds, wounds of women's hearts. He provided visions of me writing manuals for women who needed a touch, speaking encouragement to them at conferences, and even travelling globally to spread hope to these women in their own cultures.

In fall of 2009, I entered school once again to finish my Bachelor's degree and press further to earn my Doctorate in Psychology. This time, I entered with a new lens. I viewed this goal of becoming a leader in the health field as one I would successfully achieve. God pre-destined me to lead the wounded to recovery. Through my growth in the Lord, I decided not to allow an obstacle like epilepsy to hold me back from living forth His plan.

I was faced with this decision in 2004 and in 2013 when I experienced debilitating cases of seizures. Just like before, school directors recommended I leave school. My blooming faith, however, gave me the strength not to back down the second time. I knew I was planted where God wanted me and able to succeed in school. I am currently entering my second year of graduate school with a 3.75 grade point average, establishing the gift of healing God placed within me. He allowed me to endure these trials, so I may empathize with other people's pain and lead them in faith to healing.

I see a leader with empathy as one who fought battles, victoriously overcame each one, and now recognizes how to carefully guide others to success. That leader may even be currently facing a battle. However, he or she has the faith to be strengthened along the way and expects total triumph so as not to flinch when helping fellow warriors. Be comforted in knowing that God has a plan for you. Do not be discouraged by any battle you faced or allow them to hold you back in life. God promises never to give us more than we can handle. In the process of conquering these trials, we actually discover more about ourselves. We find we can move farther than before, and we are able to touch more lives. No matter how discouraging or never ending your battles may seem, do not lose faith. Though the seed may appear small, God will use your endurance to perfect, strengthen, and establish you for great and mighty things.

As mentioned at the beginning of this story, this is exactly how she penned these words. I share her story because she is no longer around. Tiffany died almost a year after she shared her story with me.

Chapter Reflections:

What were the GAP Fillers Tiffany used to determine her destination?

_____

_____

_____

How can you use those experiences to inspire you to greater purpose?

_____

_____

_____

What's one thing that you need to let go of now to open the door for greatness?

_____

_____

_____

Journal to help you process these questions in a deeper way. Schedule a quiet evening and morning to reflect further in this exercise. For deeper work on this area, you do need to work with a Life Coach. When I took the initiative to hire a life coach to help me streamline my purpose, I understood this process more clearly, and it helped me to live fully in my purpose.

PART 2
THE ABUNDANCE CYCLE -- DESIGNING YOUR PATH TO YOUR DREAM

To fulfil the beautiful dreams uncovered requires designing a clear path to follow that includes tools and a transformational team. The tools will always be there in your toolkit and available to bring tremendous success with continued use. Your transformational team of talented members will inspire and encourage you to keep your GAP filled.

CHAPTER 5
BUILD YOUR DREAM

"If you can dream it, you can do it."

~ Walt Disney

*I know what I'm doing. I have it all planned out –
plans to take care of you, not abandon you, plans to
give you the future you hope for.*

~ Jeremiah 29:11 (The Message)

Do you know that you are unique and incapable of being replaced? I discovered how irreplaceable I was in my early teen years. My life was filled with laughter, play, love, and friends, yet there was a bit of confusion in my life. Father God began to help me unravel this confusion. He assured me He was there with me all the time and He would turn my confusion into a unique story to help in the transformation of other individuals' lives. What do you do when you have dreams within your heart, yet it's filled with confusion and a lack of opportunity to release them with wings to fly? You hold them dearly in your heart, and eventually, slowly you begin to expose them one by one. Just like the game of "she loves me, she loves me not," glimpses of hope flicker in your future.

Build your dream upon hope, a feeling of expectation and desire that someday you will realize your dreams. As you journey through life, keeping hope alive will sustain your dream.

> "If you can dream it, you can do it." ~ Walt Disney

Life has been a wonderful adventure sprinkled with many challenges along the journey. Without the challenges, the fullness of life I have lived up to this point could not be attained. I came out of my mother's womb in a place that created the atmosphere for me to explore, and that I did. According to Psalm 22:9, *hope* was given to me from the time I was taken out of my mother's womb. Father God made me hope when I was upon my mother's breasts. This hope was not for only me but you also. You are unique and irreplaceable because no matter the circumstances, you have *hope*.

> You are unique and irreplaceable because no matter the circumstances, you have hope.

This *hope* given you is **H**elp, **O**pportunity, **P**erseverance, and **E**mmanuel (meaning God is with us):

- Father has given you Hope as you travel this journey of life. Who are the people who have had a lasting and positive impact throughout your life? Your best friend? Your mentor? Your accountability partner? - Your role model? These individuals are in your life for a reason. They are there to encourage, motivate, offer wisdom, unconditional love, and impact your life in a dynamic way.

- Opportunity to develop your life-giving habits and discover the gifts, talents, and skills that God has placed in you since you were first conceived. When was the last time you did a check and balance assessment of your life roles? Are they in rhythm with who you say you are? Do you know who you are? What are your values? Have you explored your strengths to help you counteract your weaknesses? It's time to take the steps to move from mediocrity to opportunity, and you can do this with the help of a skilled guide to coach you through the process.

- Perseverance to persist through the rough paths of the journey or times when you reach a plateau. Yes, when surrounded by our family, friends, mentors, and role models, we discard everything that hinders us and the sins that so easily keep us confused. It's time to run with perseverance the race marked specifically for us.

- Emmanuel, "God with us." This is our protection: one who is there with you always. This voice remains quiet until you evoke it from within. When you desire to hear from that voice, His spirit will awaken. If you pause to listen, you may hear the knocking. "Behold I stand at the door and knock". If God is for us, who can stand against us.

The time to build your dreams is now. The life cycle of the butterfly can take from one month to an entire year depending on the type of butterfly. Review the three stages of the butterfly life cycle in Chapter 3 and the Reflection Questions you completed. If you haven't completed your responses, be sure to do so before you move on so as not to hack or cut yourself off from uncovering your burning desire and living fully in your uniqueness. Your journey is determined by who you are, what you have to bring to this world, why you sense this passion, and how you plan to transform your life and the life of others.

One of my clients, let me call her Sophia, came to me with an urgency for coaching and mentoring. After spending an hour with her to go over the initial discovery process, a few things came to light. Her dreams were always shot down by a loved one. She feared she would fail if she stepped out of her comfort zone—her 9-5 job. She had a sense of loneliness though she was from a large family.

Sophia had a willingness to do the work required to renew her dreams. This is where her journey to creating a life of growth, abundance, and power began. So as not to impose my experience on her, I asked her if it was okay for me to share a bit of my story with her. This is what I shared with Sophia:

My journey to purpose began early in my life. I recall throughout my childhood and up to my young adult years how I was placed in leadership roles by my elders. I remember as far back as basic school or kindergarten, as some would call it, being in that same little church which became a school from Monday to Friday in the daytime hours. In that school I was asked to step in to lead the class when my teacher had to step out for a break, and I remembered how I totally enjoyed being given those leadership tasks.

Later in life when I was offered a job in a small advertising firm after working in several office jobs and secretarial positions, I felt that I had found my calling. I loved sales, and as I thrived in this field, friends and other leaders in the marketing world saw my exuberance and earnestly began referring and recruiting me to work for sales organizations. After giving the options quite a bit of consideration, eventually I relented, and in 1990 I joined with one of the top life insurance companies in Jamaica. This season of my life was filled with such passion and purpose. When you discover and begin to live every day doing what you love, it will cause you to soar to levels that you cannot imagine.

As a young woman in my early thirties at the time, I began working in the life insurance industry, and I could feel passion and joy every single day. In this season I established quality relationships, experienced consistent financial increase, and was the proud owner two motorcars at one time. To cap it off, I qualified as a Million Dollar Round Table (MDRT) member for three consecutive years. Since the MDRT was a prestigious club for successful financial professionals, my ego soared, and I desired more and more. This success opened up the opportunity for me to travel to the United States of America for various professional and business events, sponsored by the MDRT foundation. I was privileged to meet Dr. Ben Carson, the world renowned pediatric neurosurgeon and Les Brown, a recognized international motivational speaker and author whose message "You Gotta Be Hungry" struck a chord in my heart and stood out among other speakers' stories to challenge to us as professionals. Since then I havey become greatly motivated and inspired and have secretly desired to be on stage as an international well-known speaker one day.

Hiding your dream does not serve you. I shared this idea of becoming a speaker with a few people in my circle and ended up receiving more discouragement than encouragement. You must be careful with whom you share your dreams.

Now is the time to cut through the noise and start building your dream.

When you take the time to identify where your dream began and then explore the points in your life that ignite that dream, you will develop a map that directs you to your future. If you don't review this map regularly, you will end up giving up or losing your way.

Chapter Reflections:

What lessons in this chapter will you apply to build your dream?

_____

_____

_____

Do you have a better understanding of the timeframe and how to build it out to implement those lessons?

_____

_____

_____

CHAPTER 6
FILL IN THE GAPS WITH LOVE

"Love is the only force capable of transforming an enemy into friend."

~ Martin Luther King, Jr.

Dear friends, let us continue to love one another, for love comes from God.

~ 1 John 4:7 (NLT)

The seed of love was planted in my life beginning from as far back as I can remember being that little girl playing in our yard with my siblings and neighbours. I was always kind, forgiving even when I did not know why I was asking forgiveness, had a kind of naivety that at times was taken advantage of, but ultimately always loving and seeking love.

My yearning for love may have come from the lack thereof. From the outside one would assume that I was receiving all the love in the world that someone could have, and this I believe was the case throughout different phases of my life. It's no surprise that the lessons learned from the seeking brought me to a place of complete surrender to my Father—God.

I developed a deep love for God and in turn a deep love for who He created me to be. Having this love relationship with God is the greatest gift I have had in my life as it is what fuels me to live my best life.

> "Even when I walk through the darkest valley, I will not be afraid, for you are close beside me." ~ (Psalm 23:4)

I am always comforted by His presence and it keeps me going.

Your personal growth, abundance and power that you so long for, will require a dose of this four letter word L-O-V-E. "What's love got to do with my GAP?" Everything! Love is the catalyst to every area of your life and business. When love exudes in a genuine way from you, there is a light that shines brightly and draws others towards you and what you have to give. Commit to love unconditionally—always! Bear in mind that your first and last love is self-love, and true love comes from your Creator.

> "Dear friends, let us continue to love one another, for love comes from God."

Love yourself and others unconditionally. Love will lead you to know your value, purpose, mission, and vision for life, and it will greatly enhance your confidence. Experiencing this truth regarding love allows you to celebrate when the dreams of those in your circle come to life. Are you struggling to offer pure love to others?! Read 1

Corinthians 13: 1-13 and then personalize verses 4-8, as I have done here and let it be your daily confession.

> *I suffer long and am kind; I do not envy; I do not parade myself, I am not puffed up; I do not behave rudely, I do not seek my own way, I am not provoked, I think no evil; I do not rejoice in iniquity, but I rejoice in the truth; I bear all things, I believe all things, I hope all things, I endure all things. I never fail.*
> ~ (I Corinthians 13:4-8 NKJV)

To walk in love, you need to eradicate unforgiveness completely. You MUST make every effort to remove it from your heart, mind, speech, and life. Take stock of whether or not you are harbouring bitterness against anyone, no matter the circumstances. It's time to clean house. Do you notice that when you clean your own home or office of clutter how much better you begin to function in life? You will find much more peace and joy that fuels you to create greater success for those you serve and for yourself.

The work you have to do requires much strength and love and joy works well together. I love the verse which reminds me that "the joy of the Lord is my strength." (Nehemiah 8:10)

Make love your greatest aim. It is not easy to give kindness to others without love. When you have received God's love and mercy, regardless of your shortcomings and failings, you are required to do the same for others. You should treat them as you were treated so the love circle can grow and expand. This is what I am talking about when I say make love your greatest aim. When you keep unforgiveness in your heart, you break the circle of love, disrupting its expansion. Loving is forgiving. . . It's time to journal.

Chapter Reflections:

Go to your journal and share those thoughts in your heart on the topic of love discussed in this chapter or write your notes below:

_____

_____

_____

_____

_____

_____

_____

_____

CHAPTER 7
GAP FILLERS

"Gratitude is the healthiest of all human emotions. The more you express gratitude for what you have, the more likely you will have even more to express gratitude for."

~ Zig Ziglar

For everything there is a season, and a time for every matter under heaven:
a time to be born, and a time to die;
a time to plant, and a time to pluck up what is planted;
a time to kill, and a time to heal;
a time to break down, and a time to build up;
a time to weep, and a time to laugh;
a time to mourn, and a time to dance;
a time to cast away stones, and a time to gather stones together;
a time to embrace, and a time to refrain from

embracing;
a time to seek, and a time to lose;
a time to keep, and a time to cast away;
a time to tear, and a time to sew;
a time to keep silence, and a time to speak;
a time to love, and a time to hate;
a time for war, and a time for peace.

~ Ecclesiastes 3:1-8 (RSV)

As far as I can remember, the desire to create a lasting legacy was always in the forefront of my mind. I desired to make something of my life, establish a great career, get married and have children, own a family home and business, and contribute to the growth of leaders. With the many struggles and challenges along my path to purpose, I sometime felt I would not be able to achieve my goals and dreams. In the process I have experienced many stops and starts and learned valuable lessons from being naive or lacking maturity. My desire to impact the lives of others was the greatest propelling force.

In the Bible we are urged to "Do nothing from selfish ambition or conceit, but in humility count others more significant than yourselves." When you are divinely guided, you can be assured that your successes will be directly connected to your divine life design. Be careful of the ego here and endeavor to stay grounded by anchoring to the one who truly knows who you are. You cannot do anything without your Creator. Remember this and aspire to maintain a spirit of humility at all times.

Do not forget the efforts of those on your design team, those in your home office and on your virtual team. They all need to be recognized equally. It is quite easy to forget that you are nothing without the breath that was breathed into you by God. It would not have been possible to accomplish all you have without this ability to breathe. Consistently maintain a spirit of humility. Here is a short comical story that illustrates this point.

"A man received a promotion to the position of Vice President of the company he worked for. The promotion went to his head, and for weeks on end he bragged to anyone and everyone that he was now VP. His bragging came to an abrupt halt when his wife, so embarrassed by his behaviour, said, "Listen Bob, it's not that big a deal. These days everyone's a vice president. Why they even have a vice president of peas down at the supermarket!"

Somewhat deflated, Bob rang the local supermarket to find out if this was true. "Can I speak to the Vice President of peas please?" he asked, to which the reply came: "of fresh or frozen?"

~ Anonymous

I am amazed and proud of those individuals whom I have coached. Some of them have taken the results from their coaching sessions and have created successes far beyond themselves or my coaching. I am forever grateful to have been a part of their journeys and will always be one of their biggest cheerleaders. I will always be grateful to those who referred my services to others. Thank you for your vote of confidence. You believed in me and the work I do, and you passed on your

"Gratitude is the healthiest of all human emotions. The more you express gratitude for what you have, the more likely you will have even more to express gratitude for." ~ Zig Ziglar

experience and recommendation to others whose lives I have had the privilege to impact.

Over the years; virtual assistants, administrative professionals, and organizers have been there to help bring my thoughts and ideas to life. They make me look good, and I truly appreciate and value their work. Sometimes you may have challenges with those with whom you are aligned, but it is important to recognize their value and focus on the goodness they brought into your life, whether through a job well done or lesson learned. Your life is influencing those around you, whether you are aware of it or not. What you need to affect other's lives is right in your hands at your fingertips.

Answer the Influence Legacy Assessment questions below before continuing. Be honest and begin to list the kind of legacy you want to leave in this world there. Write down thoughts that will lead you to greater growth and development in your life and those you are called to influence.

Influence Legacy Assessment
(Answer the following questions):

Do you have influence? Describe what that looks like currently.

_____

_____

_____

What does it mean for you to be a leader?

_____

_____

_____

What leadership roles have you held in your career, ministry, or business?

_____

_____

_____

How will you lead in the future?

_____

_____

_____

What type of influence legacy do you want to leave in this world?

_____

_____

_____

Are there people in your life that you have disregarded or disconnected with since you saw them move to a better place or receive greater favor?

_____

_____

_____

From here on out, how will you treat those on your team or in your circle to give more credibility to who they are and what they have contributed to your life?

_____

_____

_____

CHAPTER 8
HONOR YOUR IMAGE

"Stop chasing the money and start chasing the passion."

~ Tony Hsieh

"Be you transformed by the renewing of your mind, that you may prove what is good, and acceptable, and perfect..."

- Romans 12:2 (King James Version)

Are you giving yourself the opportunity to recognize and appreciate the fullness of who you are?

Do you celebrate your birthdays, anniversaries, holidays?

The most important question is, "Do you celebrate you?"

It is vital for you to develop rituals and practices that honor your mind, body, and spirit by focusing on your deepest needs. Don't forget your wants. This will lift your spirit and bring a reverence to your everyday living: A quiet walk on a trail, or along the beach. Sitting quietly by a stream or river. Taking a short or long hike. Going for a bike ride. Reading a book. Praying. Dancing. Listening to a mindful podcast or your favorite music. Calling a long lost great friend.

Now it's your time to add to this list your ritual or practice or choose one of the ones listed her and begin to incorporate in your daily life.

Focus on the goodness in your life. Yes, there are bad and sometimes really horrible circumstances going on all around you, but focus on the good. I know I am dating myself here, but I am reminded of a Polaroid camera I had some twenty years ago. When I was taking a picture, only what I focused on developed in the picture regardless of all that was outside that frame. I chose what I wanted to experience, and the beauty or joy of that moment continues each time I view that picture. When you focus on the goodness in your life you decide what will bring beauty and joy. You can do when you look in the mirror at yourself and your circumstances.

In June 2018, after returning to Canada from visiting my parents in Jamaica, I received news that my father had died. Though I anticipated his imminent death, it was still a shock to me and conflicting emotions of disbelief, anger, and indifference immediately enveloped me. The relationship with my father has been distant for a number of years, even before he divorced my mother some twenty plus years ago. My mother, siblings, and I reached out to each other to process my father's death through Facebook Messenger calls, phone calls, text messages, and inspirational resources. This season has been quite a rollercoaster of emotions for us: tears, disbelief, recollecting fond and not so fond memories. Most of all, feeling comforted that he is no longer in pain, and his spirit is free. *Rest in peace Papa.*

Approaching the unplanned events in life with a deep sense of peace can carry you through the most emotional, physically, or spiritually demanding times. Cultivating an attitude of joy and peace will bring such deep-felt happiness grounded in who you authentically are. Taking this position will naturally fill up your life with abundance and power.

> "Stop chasing the money and start chasing the passion."
> ~ Tony Hsieh

One book I strongly recommend is *As a Man Thinketh* by James Allen, who talks about how your thoughts influence your results in life. He explains we are where we are in life because of our thoughts, and if we are in an unpleasant situation, we have the power to change our circumstances by changing our thoughts. He concludes we are the directors of our lives and masters of our thoughts.

Having read this book several times since I was introduced to it back in the 1980s at a Dale Carnegie course I attended, the ideas conveyed are more vital to me today because they help me to decipher the numerous messages coming from social media, the news, and other voices in my sphere of influence every day. Some of these voices in social media are in opposition to your life values, and they create a greater need for you to closely monitor your thoughts. Be sure to get a copy for yourself and read and assess how it helps you in your life and business.

In the book *The Perfect You* by Dr. Caroline Leaf she tackles the concept of 'there is only one you' from the theological, philosophical, and scientific angles. The goal here is to challenge you to think deeper about who you are and equipping you to apply the insights to your daily life.

Here is a reminder to be intentional in honoring your image so you can celebrate every day of your life. These three priceless nuggets below comes from John Maxwell book *Intentional Living*.

"The greatest way to live with honor in this world is to be what we pretend to be". ~ Socrates

1. Discover your 'Why'

According to Maxwell, "There are two great days in a person's life. The day they are born and the day they discover why." This point is quite self-explanatory and clearly expressed. You will never be truly happy until you have at least one purpose in life that absolutely drives you. It may be spending time with and providing what's best for your family, mentoring or coaching others, working to fulfill the mission of your favorite non-profit organization, or authoring the next great *New York Times* bestseller. Whatever that driving force is, once you find it, you know. It is not based on what others are doing, but it's based on what you were innately created to accomplish in this world.

2. Become a Lifelong Learner

Growth is not an automatic process. You don't automatically get better. As a lifelong learner, I get to offer greater value to my family, friends, and clients. As a speaker, trainer, and coach I have continued to apply my learning over the past few decades and continue in that role today. You must be willing to work at becoming better. People are waiting for you to show up. As you learn, you grow, and as you grow, you lead. You cannot pretend to care about your own growth. It will not be bestowed upon you just by staying alive. Your growth must be an intentional effort. I finished reading over three books this past week. *Rise and Grind* by Daymond John, *The War of Art* by Steven Pressfield, and *Elixir Project* by Kary Oberbrunner. When I read, my mind processes the events of my life more soberly. Reading provides perspectives that bring new knowledge and transformation to your existence. Take time to delve into some of your favorite topics through books. Your entire being will thank you for it.

3. Pay it Forward

Selfishness and significance are incompatible. Helping others has to be in the forefront if we want to achieve significance. Recently I read this "pay-it-forward" story about a fatherless boy and his twenty dollar gift at Aplus.com. "After finding a $20 bill in the parking lot of a Cracker Barrel, 8-year-old Myles Eckert did what few kids his age or even adults much older than he would do. He gave it to another customer he spotted — a soldier, Lt. Col. Frank Dailey — with this note: "Dear Soldier, my dad was a soldier. He's in heaven now. I found this 20 dollars in the parking lot when we got here. We like to pay it forward in my family. It's your lucky day! Thank you for your service. Myles Eckert, a gold star kid."

Needless to say, Dailey was touched by the gesture and it didn't take long for it to go viral. After a CBS story on Myles was shared via email and social media over half a million times, he was invited to appear on the *Ellen* TV show and visit with former President George W. Bush at his presidential library. A year later, his family is spearheading a nonprofit organization called the Power of 20 with the goal of giving on an even greater scale to charities and families in need — all with the help of everyday citizens inspired by Myles' one small but great act." When you give to a greater cause, you are paying it forward. If you are a tither, give a tenth of your gross earnings. You can expect "pressed down, shaken together, running over" blessings in your life. The blessings are not the focus. Look at the result

I feel compelled to share this other story. It's one I found doing a Google search some years ago. This story is of an elderly Chinese woman had two large pots. Each pot hung on the ends of a pole, which she carried across her shoulders. Every day, she used this device to carry water to her home.

One of the pots was perfect and always delivered a full portion of water. The other had a deep crack in it and leaked. At the end of the long walk from the stream to the house, the cracked pot arrived only half full.

For a full two years this situation occurred daily, with the woman bringing home only one and a half pots of water. Of course, the perfect pot was proud of its accomplishments, but the poor cracked pot was ashamed of its own imperfection and miserable that it could only do half of what it had been made to do.

After two years of what it perceived to be bitter failure, the cracked pot spoke to the woman one day by the stream, saying, "I am ashamed of myself because this crack in my side causes water to leak out all the way back to your house."

The old woman smiled and replied, "Did you notice that there are flowers on your side of the path but not on the other pot's side? I have always known about your flaw, so I planted flower seeds on your side of the path, and every day while we walked back home, you watered them and made them grow. For two years, I have been able to pick these beautiful flowers to decorate the table and give to my friends and neighbors. Without you being just the way you are, there would not have been this special beauty to grace our homes and lives."

Sometimes, it's the "cracks," or what we perceive as imperfections that create something unexpected and beautiful. These "cracks" allow something to change and ultimately make the whole much richer and more interesting. Everything and every being has its own unique purpose and destiny to fulfill.

Reflecting on your own life, how will you begin to pay-it-forward today? With or without cracks?

_____

_____

_____

_____

_____

_____

_____

_____

_____

PART 3
POWER YOUR DREAM --
7 INTENTIONAL STEPS

To maintain growth, abundance, and power in keeping your GAP filled requires fearless, self-assured, confident steps to maintain the life of growth, abundance and power you were created with.

Apply these Seven Intentional Steps Daily to keep your GAP filled.

CHAPTER 9
MAP OUT YOUR GAP

"You can map out a fight plan or a life plan, but when the action starts, it may not go the way you planned, and you're down to your reflexes – that means your [preparation:]. That's where your road-work shows. If you cheated on that in the dark of the morning, well, you're going to get found out now, under the bright lights."

~ Joe Frazier

"Suppose one of you wants to build a tower. Won't you first sit down and estimate the cost to see if you have enough money to complete it?"

~ Luke 14:28 (Revised Standard Version)

If you read no other chapter, be sure to read this one. It contains the seven steps to create your life of Growth,

Abundance, and Power. You don't want to miss a step. Do you know what happens when you miss your step? You fall. You can get hurt, sometimes a minor scratch; other times it can be something critical like a broken bone. Pace yourself as you take these steps and be sure to fully complete each one carefully.

To step into intentional living requires consistent use of your tools. Using them will be the catalyst to move you forward into the Creator's plan for your life. One foundational tool I use and confidently recommend is The Bible, along with other books that relate to my field of expertise. A few times I will venture to read a work of fiction or two which is quite rare.

I recommend that you make The Bible your main source to guide you in all you say and do. It is packed with practical ways to live your life, sharing how to treat one another, and offering affirmations of who you are, and giving answers to many of your life questions. This guide is the most powerful tool I have used throughout my life. I may not go back to many of the books I have read, but this one I read or recall from memory every day. Each year I choose to do specific readings throughout the year to help my spirit grow. I know when my spirit grows, my life goals will grow even more. I use this resource to guide my life. It reinforces who I am, why I was created, and how to pursue my purpose. These instructions are all laid out in that manual for me. I take it in daily. The Bible teaches ways to behave as individuals as well as matters of the family, community, church, and government affairs, work life, and so much more. Take time to explore this book to research and understand your reason to be alive. It's important to find a system to help ensure that you hold the word of God as sacred.

I also highly recommend networking, especially in your community. When you network with others face-to-face, in private forums, and on social media you will find your motivation increases and your productivity expands.

Growth, Abundance, and Power will be yours if you carefully take the time to map out your GAP before you begin the journey to an empowered life. This personal discovery process will help clarify how to take the next your steps into your future. These seven steps for creating a life of Growth, Abundance and Power have the following objectives:

- Unlock the secrets hidden in your hurt and pain
- Discover power moves to uncover significant experiences in your past that can fill your GAP and not drain it.
- Encourage you by reinforcing how your Creator has been at work in your life in ways perhaps unknown, fulfilling His purposes and shaping your destiny
- Awaken your dreams, design a path, and take the actions to bridge the GAP in your life.
- Provide you with a process for clarifying your future direction.
- Equip you to better empower those whom you lead.
- You will:
- Evaluate your past by developing your timeline
- Dream into your future by picturing what your future may look like
- Provide with distinctive insight into understanding your hurts and pain experienced up to this point in your life

- Uncover, discover, and process your life traumas that direct you to fill your GAP and improve your life in all areas.

> "Suppose one of you wants to build a tower. Won't you first sit down and estimate the cost to see if you have enough money to complete it?"
> ~ Luke 14:28

The ultimate goal is to discover the unique work you were created to accomplish in your life and then challenge yourself to live out your purpose with passion.

Seven Steps to Map out your GAP:

1. Step One – Creating Your Life Story
2. Step Two – Completing GAP Analysis
3. Step Three – Removing The Boulders
4. Step Four – The Surrendering Exercise
5. Step Five – Completing Your Values Audit
6. Step Six – Developing Your GAP Statement
7. Step Seven – Developing Your Personal Vision
Conclusion – Finalizing Your GAP Plan

Step One: Creating Your Life Story

The most powerful leadership tool you have is your own example. ~ John Wooden

Most important is aligning yourself to your story. Your life and journey are unique. It is a personal one! We each have a specific contribution to make in this world. Have you become so preoccupied with the living of life that you fail to see how it has been shaping up throughout the years?

Here you will begin to discover, clarify, and experience a fresh sense of purpose giving you a fresh sense of hope. Jeremiah 29:11 affirms, "For I know the plans I have for you," declares the Lord, "plans to prosper you and not to harm you, plans to give you a hope and future." If you are going through a dark time take this promise and let it be the focus of a brighter hope and future. Take time to remember to allow the past to speak to the future. In this step of the process you will take begin to write an outline of your life journey. This exercise will give you a glimpse of your life and how you are being shaped into that person you have longed to be.

Pull out your journal and begin this process of use the worksheet in the back of this book titled "Creating Your Story"

Instructions to guide you:

Search for "Dear Younger Me" by MercyMe on YouTube. Play this song a few times before writing. Time yourself for fifteen minutes. Reflection: Look at yourself ten years from today and talk to your future self ten years from now.

If you are struggling with the exercise above, here is another option. We all have a story. Your story is filled with life experiences--some good and some challenging--stories of victories and others of lessons learned. These stories all have contributed to who we are today. What's your story?

Write a 3-5 page summary of your life and journey. Before you begin writing, brainstorm some main events that have occurred in your life.

- First, write a random list of these events
- Then go back and arrange them in chronological order

- Fill in anything you remember as you put the events in order
- You are now ready to put these events of your life in story form

Do not force yourself to write a perfect story by including everything. Just write what comes to mind, and challenge yourself to be open and honest; include both the positive and negative events. As you begin composing your story details and events will come rushing back uncovering incidents you have not thought about for years.

Here are some events to jog your memory:

- Graduation, new job, school incident, moves to a new city, etc.
- People who influenced and shaped your life
- Friends, families, pastors, classmates, spouses, church members, etc.
- Incidents or statements made about you before your birth
- Childhood experiences, conflict with parents, jobs held, and places lived, etc.

Use your journal to chronicle your story or use the designated pages at the end of this book.

Step Two: Completing Your GAP Analysis

Not even analysis, by itself, can transform you. You must still do the changing yourself. ~ Natalie Wood

Your personal and professional success is a direct reflection of how you assess the pit-stops along the journey.

It's in your best interest to put your "right" skills and gifts in the place to enhance and sustain your purpose. It is essential to recognize that your best is not what's on paper but your continuous personal growth.

The study of over 1,000 historical, Biblical, and contemporary leaders, who have finished their lives well, reveals that one key to finishing well is maintaining a lifetime perspective. One example of such a leader is Joseph. His brothers stripped him of his clothes, threw him in a pit, and then sold him as a slave to a group of people called the Ishmaelites. You can read the rest of the story in Genesis 37:23-28 and draw some lessons from Joseph to gauge your growth.

This step builds upon Step One: Create Your Life Story exercise that you previously completed, and it leads you through the fashioning of your Post-It-Note timeline exercise. This is an invaluable tool first introduced to me in a Leader Breakthrough coaching session. Let it guide you to see a greater picture to outline your history. In this step you will think about significant people, events, and life experiences that have shaped your life. Put these events into chronological order, and then identify three to five segments that help to label your history.

- **Action 1**: Yellow
  - Brainstorm significant people, life experiences and events that have shaped your life. Listen to that still small voice in your heart and mind and record what is being revealed to you about your past
- **Action 2**: Pink
  - Identify painful memories
- **Action 3**: Blue
  - Create chapters

Tools needed: poster board, post-it-note pads (yellow, pink, blue, & green) permanent markers, straight edge or ruler.

Step Three: Removing The Boulders

"The major problem is that people are aware of their conscious beliefs and behaviors, but not of subconscious beliefs and behaviors. Most people don't even acknowledge that their subconscious mind is at play when the fact is that the subconscious mind is a million times more powerful than the conscious mind and that we operate 95 to 99 percent of our lives from subconscious programs...

Your subconscious beliefs are working either for you or against you, but the truth is that you are not controlling your life because your subconscious mind supersedes all conscious control. So when you are trying to heal from a conscious level–citing affirmations and telling yourself you're healthy–there may be an invisible subconscious program that's sabotaging you."

~ Dr. Bruce Lipton

I have learned from life is that it's one thing to know that all power and all answers lie within but a totally separate thing to access all of this power and inner wisdom.

Jeremiah 17:5-8 (English Standard Version) states,

"Thus says the LORD: "Cursed is the man who trusts in man and makes flesh his strength, whose heart turns away from the LORD. He is like a shrub in the desert, and shall not see any good come. He shall dwell in the parched places of the wilderness, in an uninhabited salt land. Blessed is the man who trusts in the LORD, whose trust is the LORD. He is like a tree planted by water, that sends out its roots by the stream, and does not fear when heat comes, for its leaves remain green, and is not anxious in the year of drought, for it does not cease to bear fruit"

This scripture contrasts the man who trusts in himself with the man who trusts in God.

Your subconscious mind is a very powerful and mysterious force. It can either hold you back in life or help you advance confidently in the direction of your dreams, goals, and intentions. In order for this powerful force to work with you, and for you, rather than against you, you first need to learn how to remove those hidden subconscious-self-limiting blocks, negative thoughts, feelings, and emotions that were largely formed in your mind before the age of six.

You will experience times of heat and drought in your personal and professional life. A portion of that experience will produce or yield times of pain and hurt. Your response is not to worry. Pain and negative experiences are never fun. You will often wonder about the meaning of these experiences.

This step of removing boulders will help deepen your spiritual relationship with the Creator to trust His guidance, even through the most difficult of the unveiling moments. Some of your significant life forming happens during these painful moments. John Eldridge in *Sacred Romance* encourages you to "own your woundedness or risk inflicting it onto others." In this process you will reflect on your PINK Post-it notes and begin to identify how your life experiences are used to shape you. More than likely you may still need some healing in the near future.

Take a few moments to reflect on past experiences (PINK post-it notes) and journal, reflect on what's going on inside you and the lessons there are for you to learn. Write 1 – 4 lessons learned on the GREEN Post-it notes.

Time of Reflection/Removing The Boulders Exercise

Think about what you might be experiencing in your current situation. Is there still a need for healing to occur? Take a moment and complete the following grief map to help process any grief that may require further healing

GRIEF MAP
Check any words related to your past or present pain/grief.

Abuse	Cancer	Money problems	Natural disaster
Accident	Carjacking	Panic attacks	Rape
Adoption	Death	Fired	Probate
Affair	Death - unsaved friend	Flasher	Rebellious child
AIDS	Depression	Gang-related situation	Relocation
Alcohol-related event	Discrimination	Gunshot	Retardation
Anorexia	Disease	Handicap	Retirement

Appearance	Disowned	Harassment	School dropout
Bankruptcy	Deafness	Heart attack	Separation
Battering	Divorce	Hijacking	Sexual problems
Betrayed	Drug-related issue	Illness	Stillborn child
Blindness	Dying	Incest	Stroke
Broken dream	Empty nest	Infertility	Suicide
Bulimia	Insomnia	Injury	Surgery
Burglarized	Jail term	Laid off	Unemployment
Business failure	Jilted	Loss of friendship	Unwanted pregnancy
Teen runaway	Military Separation	Loss of home	Weight-related issue
Torn family	Miscarriage	Loss of limb	Other:
Other:	Other:	Other:	Other:

- What wounds are still open?
- What issues did you check or write?
- Which experiences do you feel you have worked through and
- healed from?
- What has been your worst pain or ache?
- How did you answer the question, "What wounds are still open?"
- What questions or thoughts do you have about how you might want to recycle your grief?
- How are you doing with this topic?

Step Four — Completing Surrender Exercise

"Some of us think holding on makes us strong; but sometimes it is letting go." ~ Hermann Hesse

Before you complete this next step, pause to reflect on what might hold you back. All of us have been at this place before. Exercises like these fall prey to "good intentions" because of recurring struggles. This exercise will lead you through a time of identifying what could hold you back.

Preparation

To prepare your mind and heart to be ready for this exercise, play the popular hymn "I Surrender All." Find a quiet space where you won't be disturbed and when settled, play this song to set the atmosphere. You can find this song on YouTube at this link: Song: I Surrender All

> *"Strip down, start running — and never quit! No extra spiritual fat, no parasitic sins.*
>
> *Keep your eyes on Jesus, who both began and finished the race we're in." (Message)*
>
> *And throwing off everything that hinders us and especially the sin that so easily entangles us, let us keep running with endurance the race set before us, (ISV)*
>
> *Hebrews 12:1-2*

Place an X on the line to mark where you are right now. **My life right now is…**

_____

Not Surrendered At All   Totally Surrendered

This exercise is between you and your Creator. I am here to encourage you, not to judge you.

Check next to each area or add any other areas of your life that you have already surrendered to your Creator or are ready to surrender now.

Personal Life
Financial
Social/Relational
Mental (Abilities, Degrees/Education, Dreams, Conflicts, etc.)
Physical (Abuse-Physical or sexual, Healing, Vanity, etc)
Emotional
Family
Spiritual Growth and Faith
Spiritual Disciplines and Practice
Church Involvement (Leadership role, Ministry, Spiritual gifts, etc)
Sins/Character Faults
Addictions, Compulsions, and Obsessions
Career or Job
Other _____
Other _____

What areas of your life do you need to surrender most? I mostly want to surrender TODAY _____
_____

Pray silently. Later do surrender walk, journal, meditate or connect with your prayer partner for accountability.

Scripture Application for surrender exercise: *Jeremiah 29:11; Psalm 37:23; Proverbs 16:9; Proverbs 1:33; Proverbs 3:5; Isaiah 48:17; Psalm 32:8; Psalm 48:14; Isaiah 58:1; Jeremiah 10:23; Psalm 37:4,7*

Well Done. *(Be sure to complete this exercise before moving any further along this process)*
Your willingness to face the issues that could hold you back and to surrender them brings greater clarity and focus to complete the rest of the journey. Surrendering to the Creator continually as you journey this life opens up greater revelation about the future for your life.

Step Five – Completing Values Audit

"Success is when I add value to myself. Significance is when I add value to others." ~ *John Maxwell*

What are Values?

Values help us determine what to do and what not to do. Knowing your values helps to ground you and provides a proper perspective to make the right choices for life and business.

Who are some of the individuals whom you admire, and what are their values?

Complete the personal values audit below to help you explore and discover your own personal value.

Why are Personal Values important to you?

Your personal values are discovered by looking inside. Taking the time to look inside requires focus, discipline, and consistency. Understanding the positive implications of this exercise will come from taking time to schedule it in to your life and persevering to keep it going.

You already own these values. They are not what you plan to purchase or acquire in the future.

Why a Values Audit?

The values-discovery process examines personal values held by an individual. In 2004-2005 I spent six months working with three small business firms in Virginia as a part of a research project. First, I collected data. Secondly, I presented a proposal and workshop. Thirdly, I conducted the Values Audit with more than thirty individuals. I have since been facilitating these values audits in my workshops and online self-study courses.

Values discovery begins at the individual or personal level and communicates what is unique to the individual.

Now it is time to complete your Values Audit.

Values Audit Exercise:

- List the names of five people whom you admire (they can be living or historical, fictional or real).
- Beside each name, write down the qualities you admire in each one on your list.

For Example: Mother Teresa -- compassionate, generous, unconditional love.

Look at some of the lessons from the past and draft your 4-6 most important core values.

Values are core convictions and preferences that have developed from your past journey. Life values are signposts from your past that can provide direction and pointers into your future.

Now choose 1-6 values learned in your Timeline and use Green Post-it-Notes to label each section.

Values Audit Exercise:

Name	Qualities You Admire

Here is an example of my Value Statement:

Dr. Hopelyn values faith, family, purpose, integrity, accountability, and legacy. She values her trust in God, investing time and energy in those whom she is closest to, living with intentionality, living above reproach, having trusted guides in her life, and making a difference that lasts beyond her lifetime. Her most powerful driving force is her passion to see professionals and entrepreneurs live the way God intended them to in life and business.

Below is a list of individual core values to jog your memory as you process your values.

INDIVIDUAL CORE VALUES CHECKLISTS/ LIST OF VALUES:

Achievement
Accountability
Commitment
Compassion
Consistency
Credibility
Creativity
Concern for others
Dependability
Excellence

Empowerment
Growth
Reward
Honesty/Integrity
Loyalty
Leadership
Performance
Recognition
Quality
Teamwork

Reconciliation
Religion
Trust
Change
Security
Love
Reaching out
Service to others
Responsiveness
Stewardship

Step Six – GAP Statement

"Definiteness of purpose is the starting point of all achievement." ~ W. Clement Stone

We are all here for a reason, so get some inspiration to find yours from this step about living a life of Growth, Abundance, and Power.

Your GAP statement is one of being -- it's not about what you do but who you are. Your Growth-Abundance-Power started before you even existed. You were created with all the faculties needed to seek out knowledge that would lead to your growth. Abundance is in your DNA. All you need for living a successful life is at your command. "Ask and it shall be given, seek and you shall find, knock and the door shall be open unto you"

Developing a GAP statement will give you a better understanding of who you are and why you exist.

Growth, Abundance, and Power are a dynamic trio when you understand how they combine to become a mighty force to be reckoned with. This statement will give clarity to your reason for existence. Wrapped in this statement is your life's purpose and vision. It will help to inspire your empowerment.

In this step of the process, you will first seek out scriptural and/or inspirational quotes that you have previously used to guide your life in the past up until now. Next, you will review mandates given from leaders whom you admire in your area of interest. Once you complete these steps, you will draft a two to three sentences for your GAP statement.

GAP Statement Exercise

Personal Reflection

The words in Psalm 119:105 and following describe the Word of God as a lamp unto our feet and a light unto our path. A lamp supplies temporary lighting and gives guidance and hope for the immediate time. Light provides direction and courage for the future.

What scriptures or quotes have given you guidance, encouragement, direction, hope, and courage in your life? What type of environment causes you to thrive? What's your definition of abundance?

List those verses and quotes, then summarize them along with your insight to the questions above.

Scripture/Quote Verse	Significance

Example Statement

Scriptures/Quotes:

- Let your roots grow down into him, and let your lives be built on him. Then your faith will grow strong in the truth you were taught, and you will overflow with thankfulness. Colossians 2:7 (NLT)
- So that you may live a life worthy of the Lord and please Him in every way: bearing fruit in every good work, growing in the knowledge of God... Colossians 1:10
- Be diligent in these matters; give yourself wholly to them, so that everyone may see your progress. 1 Timothy 4:15

I will seek wisdom from my Creator so that my growth is established on a solid foundation. Intentional efforts will bring the abundance I desire to take care of my needs and diminish lack in all areas of my life. My diligence in pursuing God-given dreams will give me the courage to stand in power before kings, those in high offices, as well as the poor man on the street.

Reminder: Your GAP statement is not an extensive "to do list" of your expectations. It must be a concise description, explaining why you exist based on the verses, quotes, and questions you answered in the reflection section above.

Draft of Your GAP Statement

_____

_____

_____

_____

_____

_____

Checks for Your Statement

- Is it a statement of being, more than doing?
- Is it a reflection of who you are and describes you exist?
- Does it reflect the heart of your Creator and what He desires from you as His follower?
- Is it something that gives your life a sense of direction?

Spend some time re-drafting your statement into a concise 1-2 sentence statement.

Based upon your reflections and work in this session, write out your GAP statement of purpose and why you believe you exist.

Your GAP Statement

_____

_____

_____

_____

_____

_____

Step Seven – Developing Your Personal Vision

Whereas purpose was a statement of being, vision reflects doing and accomplishment. Vision is a word picture of a future reality from your Creator's perspective. It describes end results, as you live out your purpose, in the context in which He has placed you. Vision motivates. It's what gets you up at night. It reflects your best understanding to date of what you feel your Creator wants you to accomplish.

In this step of the process you will spend some personal time alone and experience a Personal Vision Retreat. Take the time here to reflect on what the next chapter of your life might look like if you were to please your Creator. Your vision statement starts in a narrative form and then becomes a more concise statement of personal vision.

Personal Vision Exercise

Personal Vision is a statement of doing. While purpose describes why you exist, Personal Vision describes what you hope to accomplish in this world. What are the action steps required to see your dreams realized? Have you written them down? Have you set a timeline for each step? Personal vision is an exercise in future perfect thinking. I remember the first time I heard this term in my doctoral studies and how far-fetched it seemed. I wondered how much can one do to determine their future? After practicing this principle over the years, I would strongly recommend it to you. It calls for discerning the influences in our past that have created your unique passion. Once you draw on them, they will guide you to accomplish your life dreams.

Purpose clarifies, but Vision motivates. It is what wakes you up, and keeps you up at night. Vision (in this exercise) is personal. It is different from that of your organization. Even if you lead an organization, personal vision is your part of the greater corporate vision.

Be reminded that you have been created to do good works, which your Creator authored into your life before time began.

4-Part Exercise:

Firstly: Review your Timeline

Look for common insights or themes that may surface in your reflection.

Think about people and circumstances that have most shaped your life and what you do today. Who are they? What did they shape you to do?

Complete the following:

- When I think about the future, I would love to give myself to _____ and concentrate on _____ because _____.

- People who know me well believe I am most effective when I am involved in _____

- From my view, the activities that allow me to make my greatest contribution in this world are

   _____

- When I have completed these tasks, I have a sense of _____

- Though I have dismissed the thought for various reasons, I sometimes feel I really should be doing _____ because ___

   _____

Secondly -- Reflection Question

As you look back over your Post-it time-line, there are defining moments or experiences that begin to shed light on your Creator's design for your life pertaining to your Growth, Abundance, and Power. It may be one event or a series of experiences that begin to point to a unique contribution. I refer to these events as GAP pointers.

Look back over your timeline and list some of the experiences and the insight you received.

Experience	Insight

Thirdly -- Your Vision Retreat

Take 30 minutes to reflect. Find a quiet place or that space you have created for journaling. Your surrender exercise completed in Step Four should have prepared you to embrace this time of reflection more fully. Listen for God's voice each time you reflect. Let Him speak into your life experiences and dreams, then journal your thoughts down.

The vision you seeded in your past reflects your "best understanding" of what is next.

Vision is a word-picture of a future reality from your Creator's perspective. Vision is much more than just dreaming up a big-dream. This Vision Retreat invites you into a time of reflection on the next chapter of your life and journey.

The Vision Retreat is a time to ask your Creator to speak, and for you to journalize your thoughts. Refining of your Vision Statement will come later. Journal around this question:

- *Based upon the way your vision has shaped up for you in your past (Timeline), what do you believe He is calling you to accomplish in the next chapter of your life to embrace the future in store for you?*
- *Or, if you knew you could not fail, what would you do to live an empowered life?*

Here are some GAP checks for what you have written above in your Journal

Can you see the GAPs?

Are the GAPs bigger than you can handle alone?

Does the GAP engage your passion? Is it anchored in your past?

Would you fill the GAP even if you did not get paid to fill it, or had to pay for the chance to fill it?

Fourthly -- Creating Your Statement of Personal Vision

Some reminders for your draft:

Vision is a statement of doing.

In your Life Purpose you summarized what your heart is calling you to be. Don't fall into the trap of re-writing your purpose and calling it vision. Vision is purpose lived out, and secondly this draft is your best understanding to date of what your God is calling you to do. It will grow and change as you continue to live it out.

Example Statements:

- As I take the steps to fill my GAP, I dedicate myself to creating...
  - A safe place within myself (personal care and growth).

- A safe place within our home (intentional time with Robin and our kids).
- A safe place with a group of friends-colleagues (transparency and accountability).
- A series of safe places for godly leaders, through the development of resources and supportive learning environments.

Another Example:

I live to speak courage, passion and faith into the lives of professionals and entrepreneurs who are committed to live an intentional life of Growth, Abundance, and Power. I will assist these leaders in discerning their commitment, calling, and contribution, accelerating their potential to fulfill their God-given destiny. I will coach/mentor these leaders to focus and live out their destiny and expand their leadership capacity.

DRAFT of My Personal Vision

Using your journal time, and reflection, draft a 2-3 sentence word picture of your personal vision on the lines below:

Finalizing Your Personal Vision Statement

Now that your statement is in draft form, it is good simply to sit with it for some time. Maybe leave it for a day or two then revisit and revise until you are happy with the final statement. Plan to review it every three to six months and update as necessary.

It is also good to have friends, spouse, and those who know you best give their feedback. Spend some time and work on drafting it into 2-3 well-crafted sentences.

Normally those who develop a well-edited statement are able to pull out one-line and use it as a tagline of the complete statement. (Example: *I help professionals and entrepreneurs identify life's challenges so they can overcome the setbacks in their lives and become empowered to live their dreams.*)

Once your editing is complete, write out your final version of your personal vision in the area below.

My Personal Vision Statement

_____

_____

_____

Conclusion – Your Personal GAP Plan Statement

Your GAP Plan Statement integrates how you will enhance your personal and professional life, extend your abundance of the money you earn and the assets you acquire, and develop your power to stand courageously in what you are called to do in this world.

This is the home stretch. You complete this process by collecting your work and weaving your spiritual purpose, core values, and personal vision into your GAP plan statement. This statement will serve both as a compass and a decision-making tool as you move into the future.

Conclusion – Your GAP Plan Statement Exercise

On a recent drive with my husband, Audley, from Maple Ridge, British Columbia, Canada to Santa Clara, California, we listened to the audio book *Rise and Grind* by Daymond John, star of ABCs *Shark Tank*. As we considered the recording, he shared about Gary Vaynerchuck, talking about situations we do and do not have control over. We began reflecting on how thankful we were for our spiritual foundation. In our lives we make plans for the future and most of the time we have to make adjustments along the journey. When we consider what we have and don't have control over, it encourages us to stay grounded in our faith with the Master Designer. We don't have control over who lives long or who dies early, but because we know who has control, there is no fear nor anxiety about the fact we have no say in the mortality of our loved ones.

Now write out your GAP Plan Statement, your blueprint, and a decision-making guide to live an empowered life. Use the guideline below to complete the process. From the previous exercises completed in this section, begin to list the action steps and goals for each action step to give you more clarity in creating your GAP Plan Statement.

Action Steps...

1st

_____

2nd

_____

3rd

_____

Goals for Action Steps...

1st

_____

    1st

_____

    2nd

_____

    3rd

_____

2nd

_____

    1st

_____

    2nd

_____

    3rd

_____

3rd

_____

    1st

_____

    2nd

_____

    3rd

_____

Complete your GAP Plan

Write out your Personal GAP Plan Statement:

Long Version:

_____

_____

_____

_____

_____

_____

_____

_____

Short Version:

_____

_____

_____

_____

CHAPTER 10
JOIN LIKE-MINDED COMMUNITIES

"Talent wins games, but teamwork and intelligence win championships."

~ Michael Jordan

Do nothing from selfish ambition or conceit, but in humility count others more significant than yourselves.

~ Philippians 2:3 (NLT)

Prior to completing my doctoral degree in Strategic Leadership in May 2005, I had been actively involved in communities and networking groups that kept me inspired and motivated to live a passionate and purposeful life. I found that after I graduated some of these groups did not offer enough support to help me move to the next level. In 2006 after a bit of research

I found a Life Purpose Coach with whom I developed a coaching relationship and after my first 10 weeks of coaching experience, decided to join the organization. This opened up the opportunity for me to become a coach trainer and maintain an accountability partnership with coaches and leaders in that organization. As an entrepreneur who worked from home, this connection helped me to stay focused and provided support for me to grow in my area of work. This relationship lasted for about 4 years when I began exploring other similar organizations that were advancing in the areas of technology and social media, keeping pace with changes in the world of coaching, speaking, and training.

By early 2016 I made the decision to align myself with the John Maxwell Team, that offered a speaking, training , and coaching certification program that is number one in the world. They are the world's largest and fastest growing leadership and entrepreneurship program. I aligned with this team where they would be helping me reach my purpose, vision and goals; maximizing my legacy; developing the power of an abundant mindset; developing strategies for success and team networking; and personal independence and income. While this is a great team with great offerings, I needed more.

In April 2018 while visioning into the next five years, I was asking God for clarity and the name Kary Oberbrunner kept coming up in several forms. In conversations with my life coach, in a teaching audio by John Maxwell, and also in my social media feeds. I decided to reach out to Kary and was inspired by the work he was doing with Igniting Souls and made the decision to join another elite team -- Author Academy Elite. This team is helping me advance my dream of helping professionals and entrepreneurs identify life's challenges so they can overcome the setbacks in their lives and become empowered to live the life of their dreams.

When you decide to take on this dream that ignites you and unearth it for personal growth, abundance, and power; you will need to align yourself with like-minded, trail-blazing, authentic, and caring individuals who will help keep that flame ignited.

> "None of us, including me, ever do great things. But we can all do small things, with great love, and together we can do something wonderful."
> ~ Mother Teresa

One key is to allow God's spirit to guide you every step of the way to be assured that you flourish in your life and work and experience success directly related to your passions and goals.

Take time to get to know people and groups to help you take your dream to the next level. As one of my mentors, John Maxwell says, "one is too small a number for greatness." How will you grow into the future? You will grow leaps and bounds when you have a trusted life coach or guide to help you navigate the rest of your life's journey.

Your life is influencing those around you whether you are aware of it or not. What type of influence legacy do you want to leave in your world?

What you need to affect other's lives is right in your hands. Complete the Influence Legacy Exercise below. **Be honest with yourself and begin to list below the kind of legacy you want to leave in this world.** This is the only way you will get your best answers that lead you to growth and development in your life and in those whom you will influence.

Influence Legacy Exercise:

_____

_____

_____

_____

_____

_____

_____

Chapter Reflections:
Have you created your Influence Legacy?

_____

_____

How does it make you feel now that it's completed?

_____

_____

_____

CHAPTER 11
KEEP A STEADY PACE

Do you see what this means—all these pioneers who blazed the way, all these veterans cheering us on? It means we'd better get on with it. Strip down, start running—and never quit! No extra spiritual fat, no parasitic sins. Keep your eyes on Jesus, who both began and finished this race we're in. Study how he did it. Because he never lost sight of where he was headed— that exhilarating finish in and with God—he could put up with anything along the way: Cross, shame, whatever. And now he's there, in the place of honor, right alongside God. When you find yourselves flagging in your faith, go over that story again, item by item, that long litany of hostility he plowed through. That will shoot adrenaline into your souls!

Hebrews 12:1

"Slow but steady wins the race."

~ Aesop

Taking risks is inevitable and the more you take risks as you journey, the farther along you will go. Taking action always require taking risks. Your dreams will never be realized if you do not take risks. When your discovery and understanding of who you are become clearer, your resolve becomes stronger because you know you are not standing in your own strength.

How did I get here?

My career with a prestigious life insurance company in Jamaica came to a halt, and I found myself at a place of immense depression. Suddenly helpless and hopeless. The doctors diagnosed me as "suffering from anxiety." During those six months of desolation, I listened to God. I could hear Him saying, "It is time to make a change. Let go."

How can God ask me to let go of something I loved so much and had finally become successful at doing? How could I make this shift? My inadequacies ran deep. My thoughts also turned to the women in leadership in my church and surrounding communities. Yes, I served them but felt so ill-equipped. This lack of confidence stemmed from unresolved issues in my past, which the job loss triggered.

I sought help and moved steadily ahead but not without a considerable amount of processing. I had also been asking God for an opportunity to return to college to become more skilled to serve. Little did I know of the future plans he had for me.

> "Lord, I'm going to hold steady on to You and You've got to see me through."
> ~ Harriet Tubman

My passion to serve through mentorship has been with me since I was a teenager. Those who aren't aware of who they are, why there were created, and what they were created to do have long tugged at my heart. I believe this deep passion came from unmet answers from my own life's journey. My dream of becoming a nurse was shattered after high school, and for twelve years I moved from job to job before I found a career that I fell in love with and became one of the most successful representatives for the company I served.

My mother became a citizen of the USA several years prior and offered me the opportunity to relocate to America. When my career at the insurance company ended, I knew it was time, but I resisted because I loved my country, Jamaica, so much.

After wrestling with God and landing in a desolate place for almost a year, I finally surrendered. It was time to follow God. I left my familiar homeland in Jamaica to come to the USA. Through a series of "God-events," I completed eleven years of education, receiving my bachelor's, master's, and doctorate degrees. If that was not enough, toward the end of the educational journey I became parent to my deceased sister's son and reconnected with my high school boyfriend, got married, and relocated to Canada.

The dream for my Jamaican sisters never left me throughout the eleven years I spent in universities. Each of my projects talked about an organization to help transform the lives of others, even though the structure of the programs and names changed on each of my projects. To help me see this dream turn into a reality I sought a Life Coach to mentor me for this next season of my life. Eventually I found Katie Brazelton of Life Purpose Coaching Centers International. Her coaching program helped me become a more confident and purposeful woman and gave me practical tools to put wings to my dream.

In 2007, Hopelyn International Network [HIN] was launched with the primary goal to reach people in my home country, Jamaica, and worldwide. Since then I have coached, trained, and hosted seminars and workshop all over Canada: Whitehorse, Yukon Territories; Creston, BC; The Lower Mainland area in the Vancouver area; and I have an online presence directed to professionals and entrepreneurs all over the world. In addition, I have been able to return to Jamaica and impact the lives of more than 1000 individuals face-to-face in the Kingston and Mandeville areas as well as by air time with local TV and Radio stations.

These accomplishments are simply the start of the journey to fulfill my dreams and vision. I am filled with faith and hope with a continued desire to change my world. I remain passionate about this God-given dream, and I awake daily to my God-given purpose. I continue to stay close to God to remain inspired. Living in my own human strength is totally impossible. My faith undergirds my purpose, my dreams, my heart to reach professionals and entrepreneurs and see their lives transformed. My burning desire to make a difference in my community, Jamaica, and the world at large continues to motivate me every day.

At this point in my life, there have been many who have contributed to my success. Recognizing the importance of partnerships, I want to mention two mentors who have impacted my life over the past five years Katie Brazelton and Dani Johnson.

My gratitude goes to Katie for embracing and taking me under her wing. She believed in me and nurtured my dreams with clarity and strength. Knowing her in person where I could spend time in her presence and receive her warm embraces have been wonderful reminders that give me great joy. Her step of faith to do all that she has done with the Pathway to Purpose series and all her new projects will continue to inspire me.

I first heard of Dani from my first Life Coaching client, and it took almost three years after hearing about her for my husband and me to attend her "First Steps to Success" Seminar in California. Her enthusiasm, love for Jesus, and ability to be successful against all odds continues to motivate me. She reminds me to NEVER give up! The dreams God has placed in my heart will be fulfilled if I don't give up on the dream.

My strength comes from relying on God and my relationship with him, to make it through whatever challenges I will face while living each day with the courage to fill my GAP--Personal growth, Abundance, and Power. Many times I have felt like giving up on the passion that keeps me alive, but building upon the foundation of who I am and whose I am keeps me going. I know that this journey is a process and not a destination. Each step along the journey the path gets brighter and brighter, and the joy I receive gives me greater strength to keep going. An affirmation I repeat often and use as a guide comes from Proverbs 3:5: Trust in the LORD with all your heart, and do not lean on your own understanding. This affirmation brings me back to centering myself spiritually, and you can also adopt it if you like.

What is stopping you from taking risks to fulfill your dreams? If you find yourself wavering in taking the bold steps required for your journey, go back and review 'Establish Your Foundation' in Chapter 3.

Spending time to be still and listen will help prepare you to receive what your Creator is saying to you.

Keep re-discovering your values, skills, gifts, and talents. Refine your purpose, mission, and vision. Align yourself with some trusted counsellors, coaches, and associates.

Chapter Reflections:

Review your GAP Assessment Exercise completed in chapter.

_____

_____

_____

What GAPs are still open?

_____

_____

_____

CHAPTER 12
LEVERAGE YOUR STRENGTHS

"I can do all things through him who strengthens me."

~ Philippians 4:13

Life takes on meaning when you become motivated, set goals, and charge after them in an unstoppable manner.

~ Les Brown

To live out your dreams you have to expect the impossible. No dream is too BIG for you to accomplish. Continue to expect the impossible. When Abraham had a problem believing the impossible, here is what God did: "Then the Lord took Abram outside and said to him, 'Look up into the sky and count the stars if you can. That's how many descendants you will have!'" (Genesis 15:5 NLT)

Write down your dreams, take pictures of your dreams, and when you begin to doubt the possibilities, refocus your attention on them and keep going towards them. Here are some inspirational and motivational quotes from some of my mentors along the purpose journey:

> *"Many persons have the wrong idea of what constitutes true happiness. It is not attained through self-gratification but through fidelity to a worthy purpose."*
> ~ Helen Keller

> *"If you want to live a happy life, tie it to a goal, not to people or things."* ~ Albert Einstein

Continue to write down your dreams on My Dream Page in the Appendix or in your personal journal. List all the dreams you have for your life, family, career, business, travel/vacations, home, and future life or retirement. When you have completed a listing all the dreams you can recall, then it is time to create some goals around them.

With the help of a Life Coach, you can get much more accountability and guidance to attain these dreams. Keep your GAP Plan close as it will provide the direction and focus to guide you along the journey. Review your GAP Plan often to help you flourish in achieving these goals. This roadmap significantly increases your chances to arrive successfully to each destination point on your journey.

According to Webster's Online Dictionary, a goal is a boundary, limit; the terminal point of a race or the end toward which effort is directed. My friend, Lynne, shared this story about a New York City architect and contractor friend who told her that whenever he has a twelv-month project to build a skyscraper, it takes nine out of those twelve months to build the foundation. Everything else takes three months: the dry walling, roof, windows, doors, wiring, and other jobs. So the foundation takes up 75% of the time to build the entire building. That is the key, we have to build a solid foundation and the rest is easy.

The first chapter of this book gave you tools to create a solid foundation. Review this chapter, if you have not already taken those first steps. When you know your values and purpose, your mission and vision become clearer. Are you being pessimistic toward your future or living a life of doubt?! It's time to change your life's story! So let your imagination go and dare to dream.

Les Brown reminds us: "Wanting something is not enough. You must hunger for it. Your motivation must be absolutely compelling in order to overcome the obstacles that will invariably come your way."

Dr. Brown's Story Continues

Tragedy strikes... My sister, Stephanie, who had been diagnosed with breast cancer in 1996 passed away in 2002. This was at the beginning of my second residency in the doctoral program. Even though this was a traumatic blow for me, I was committed to do what it took to continue and complete my degree. In the midst of it all, I also gained full custody of Stephanie's only child, Jahmarley. This blessing was not anticipated, and I am thankful every day for the opportunity to be a parent to this precious child. Was this a difficult transition? Oh yes! When Jahmarley arrived, I looked to any positive, godly resource I could find to help us survive. We both attended counseling to assist in the relationship transition and received help in dealing with the pain of losing his mother, my sister.

It was a challenging time for us both. I felt that the role of a single mother was suddenly thrust upon me and decided I needed to get

> He gives strength to the weary and increases the power of the weak." ~ Isaiah 40:29

some extra help in this area. I completed a parenting class to aid me in developing my parenting skills. I must admit there have been growing pains, but I am so grateful to have him in my life. I have watched Jahmarley grow into a well-adjusted young man. He is now 24 years old, attending Bible College, very involved in the church, youth leadership, and missions. He is a godly, well dressed young man and a great example to many in the community, both young and old. I am so proud of him. He makes all things beautiful in its time... Over the years, I had several failed relationships. These were relationships that I was hoping would lead to marriage. Now, I felt like I had come to the end of my rope and declared that "I was done with men!"

In terms of a relationship with a man, the only conditions I would change would be these: 1) This man and I must share the same kind of relationship I had with God 2) This individual must be someone I know from my past. 3) There must be shared cultural similarities with this person

Yes, I had thrown down the gauntlet, and not more than about six weeks later, I got an unanticipated call from Audley, my high school sweetheart. This was a year short of completing my doctoral program. It was a Saturday afternoon, and I had just returned from a makeover party with a group of ladies. I was overjoyed and super excited about the connections I had made that afternoon. So here I was, returning home, chatting on my cell phone with my girlfriend, and as I plopped on the chair in my home office, the home telephone rang. I was still on my cell phone so I reached over to look at the caller ID. I saw a strange number and Saskatchewan in the name section. I began pondering, "Whom do I know from Saskatchewan?" Just as I remembered that the only person I knew in that part of the world was Audley, the phone stopped ringing. I completed my call on the cell phone and then hurriedly called back the number.

This was the beginning of a whirlwind romance. Needless to say, the flickering relationship fires were rekindled, and Audley and I got married on April 16, 2005. A month later I graduated, and since that time, Audley and I have been blessed with three handsome boys whom we love with all our hearts. We have had our challenges, yet we have seen the two older boys grow up to be successful, married men, and the youngest is in college. We know our Creator had greater things in store for them all, and daily we are thankful "they are taught by the Lord, and great is their peace." We continue to pray they all grow to their highest potential and be all that God has called them to be." We are so blessed to have these young men in our lives and they are truly a blessing. Audley and I are completely happy with our family and filled with His joy daily to keep us as we pursue Hiss Divine design for our lives. Together we face challenges knowing that "His strength is made perfect in our weakness."

For many years I wrote my dreams in my journals and continually felt the strong desire to serve the professional and entrepreneurial community in a greater way. I wrote about creating a House of Hope, offering a place for the motherless and fatherless to find a sense of belonging, helping them to find their voice, helping those in leadership to become bolder and shine more brightly in the world. These were also some of my own yearnings.

After my doctoral graduation, all these dreams began to form and come to life. In 2007, Hopelyn International Network was born. This organization was in the works since 2005, and over those two years I developed and hosted workshops, taught at conferences, and sought out the help of a trusted life coaches. I have been honored to provide a service to empower those in ministry and business by giving them tools and resources to assist in the transformation of their lives from being ordinary people to being exceptional leaders. The focus of this organization is helping others discover the great individuals they were created to be to awaken their dreams. We also help them design a strategy, and do what it takes to accomplish the dream. The ultimate goal of Hopelyn International Network, is to help others embrace their life's purpose and live more courageously to bring joy and wealth in their lives and those whom they are called to serve. This is a message of HOPE, and hope is for everyone. I am an author, speaker, and leadership coach who offers training for those who have similar aspirations.

Chapter Reflections:

What are your top three strengths?

_____

_____

_____

How will you use them to leverage your future successes?

_____

_____

_____

FILL YOUR GAP
DREAM JOURNAL
GROWTH. ABUNDANCE. POWER.

Some questions to jog your mind: Who am I? What are the longings of my heart? When do I want to achieve them? Where will this desire lead me? Why am I going there? How am I hoping to achieve it? Have I mapped out the direction I will take? What does this journey say about who I am? What passion will drive me for the rest of my life?

_____

_____

_____

_____

_____

_____

REFERENCES

Scriptures were cited from the Bible using the following versions:

English Standard Version
King James Version
New Living Translation
Revised Standard Version
Contemporary English Version

Pathway to Purpose Series - Kathy Brazelton, Life Purpose Coaching Centers International

Online Resources from Leader Breakthru Training: Focused Living

Post-It Note Timeline Resources available at leader-breakthru.com

ABOUT THE AUTHOR

Dr. Hopelyn Mullings Brown is Transforming Lives. Through her writing, speaking, and coaching; she helps professionals and entrepreneurs uncover blind spots in the times of hurt and pain in their lives that can lead them on the pathway to a life of Growth, Abundance, and Power. She is the Founder of Hopelyn International Network [HIN], which serves the business and non-profit community. She and her husband Audley met in Jamaica while attending high school. They have 3 adult sons and 3 precious grandchildren. Dr. Brown is a certified member of The John Maxwell Team.

Connect at www.DrHopelyn.com

TAKE YOUR NEXT STEP

JOIN A FILL YOUR GAP COACHING COHORT

Visualize author and coach Dr. Hopelyn or one of her Certified Coaches leading you through a transformational process where you uncover blind spots in the times of trauma and pain that leads you on the pathway of Growth, Abundance and Power.

Visualize your new found confidence as you live with greater Growth, Abundance and Power.

Join other entrepreneurs and professionals who have unlocked the secrets hidden in their hurt and pain. Awaken your dreams, design a path, do the actions to bridge the GAP in your life.

You can connect from anywhere in the world.

Find out more at FillYourGAPBook.com

THE FILL YOUR GAP TEAM

Certified Speakers, Trainers, and Coaches

One is too small a number for greatness.

Team work makes the dream work.

Our tribe is growing and we call it Transform Your Life CircleUP.

If you desire to connect to a team that help individuals uncover their blocks from hurt and pain, and discover defining moments to experience beautiful dreams and awaken to inspiration for future successes, consider joining The Fill Your GAP Team. Do work you love and get paid for it. That's an intentional move!

Find out more at FillYourGAPBook.com

Join us at
THE FILL YOUR GAP
Live Event

When you decide to take on this dream that ignites you and unearth it for personal growth, abundance, and power; you will need to align yourself with like-minded, trail-blazing, authentic, and caring individuals who will help keep that flame ignited.

Join our growing Transform Your Life CircleUP tribe!

Find out more at FillYourGAPBook.com

CPSIA information can be obtained
at www.ICGtesting.com
Printed in the USA
LVHW031109141218
600394LV00005B/218/P

9 781640 854758